Bible Stories Through the Year

Also by Bob Hartman and published by Lion Hudson:

Telling the Bible
Telling the Gospel
Anyone Can Tell a Bible Story
The Lion Storyteller Bible
The Lion Storyteller Christmas Book
Easter Angels
Bible Baddies
Old Testament Tales: The Unauthorized Version
New Testament Tales: The Unauthorized Version

BIBLE STORIES THROUGH THE YEAR

Lectionary readings for Year A,
retold for maximum effect

BOB HARTMAN

MONARCH
BOOKS
Oxford, UK & Grand Rapids, Michigan, USA

Published by Monarch Books
an imprint of
Lion Hudson plc
Wilkinson House, Jordan Hill Road,
Oxford OX2 8DR, England
Email: monarch@lionhudson.com
www.lionhudson.com/monarch

ISBN 978 0 85721 329 7
e-ISBN 978 0 85721 459 1

First edition 2013

Acknowledgments
Scripture quotations taken from the Holy Bible, New International Version Anglicised. Copyright © 1979, 1984, 2011 Biblica, formerly International Bible Society. Used by permission of Hodder & Stoughton Ltd, an Hachette UK company. All rights reserved. "NIV" is a registered trademark of Biblica. UK trademark number 1448790.

A catalogue record for this book is available from the British Library

Printed and bound in the UK, July 2013, LH27.

For Lowell who gave me the idea and
Chris who lent me the lectionary

Contents

Introduction

This book is all about enjoying the Bible.

"Enjoy" is not the first word that came to mind. I thought "appreciate" or "honour" might work – but they both imply a certain distance. And this book is most definitely not about distance. It's about crawling into the text and spending time with it and savouring it.

That's a good word – savouring. Because to savour, you have to taste. And that's about as "up close and personal" as you can get. But it's still not quite right – largely because God's Word isn't "savour-y". It's sweet! At least that's what Psalm 119:103 says – sweeter than honey, in fact. And I don't know about you, but I've got a bit of a sweet tooth! I enjoy what's sweet – in both the culinary and colloquial sense of the word.

We're back where we started. This book is about enjoying the Bible. But enjoying it – tasting its sweetness – in a particular context. A public context. An out-loud context. A community context. The contexts, as it happens, in which much of the Bible was originally shared. Publicly, out loud, in community. As a part of worship.

Sadly, much of our experience of hearing the Bible read in that context is anything but sweet:

Sometimes the Bible is read with little enthusiasm – dry as a three-day-old scone.

Sometimes there's not quite enough preparation – like an undercooked egg.

Sometimes it's like fast food – rushed through with no time to dwell on the meaning.

And sometimes it's just boring – like, I don't know, like turkey leftovers (not again!) five days after Christmas.

I concluded my book *Anyone Can Tell a Bible Story* with a chapter on Reading the Bible. And in that chapter, I suggested that an effective Bible reading requires preparation – understanding the meaning of the passage and the nature of the text (is it narrative, poetry, epistle?). It also requires practice (more than a quick skim during the notices), and creativity (are there characters who need bringing to life?).

That kind of reading, which comes from time spent with the text – understanding it, tasting it (and, yes, savouring it!) – benefits both the reader and the congregation and brings us to a place where we look forward to that moment when God's Word is read. When we enjoy it!

There are many different ways to read the text, a whole variety of techniques that will help us to enjoy it. And that's what this book attempts to illustrate. I have taken two readings from each week or special day from the *Revised Common Lectionary* and have suggested a fresh way to present those readings.

Sometimes that involves one, two, or more readers at the front. Sometimes it involves the congregation, or different groups within the congregation. Sometimes it's a retelling or rewording of the text (and, yes, there is inevitably some degree of interpretation in every retelling or rewording). Sometimes it uses the actual Bible text. Sometimes there are actions. Sometimes there are even a few stage directions. Sometimes the reading is aimed at adults. Sometimes at the children. But in every case, my hope is that the suggestions I make will help the readers and the congregation to better understand and appreciate the *meaning* of the text and also to enjoy the experience of *hearing* it (although, for many of these readings, there's a lot more than "hearing" going on).

For those of you who already use the lectionary, the way the book is set out will be familiar territory. It simply follows the readings in Year A. For those of you who do not use the lectionary, there is a Scripture index at the back of the book so you can find readings that fit the themes of your sermons and services.

Just as an aside, if you have never used the lectionary, it is a very freeing experience. I come from a tradition where we don't commonly use it either, and the word "freeing" does sound that bit counter-intuitive. Isn't it more freeing to preach from those passages you like or are led to? Well, sometimes, yes. But having committed myself to using the lectionary from time to time in my preaching career, I have discovered that the lectionary actually does *free* me from my own set of "pet" scriptures and themes and forces me to deal with passages I might never have preached from. Some of those sermons have been my best sermons, I think, and have stretched me as a preacher and a believer.

In the lectionary there are obviously more readings allocated for each week than I have covered, and some of you may be frustrated that you did not find the passage in a certain week that you were hoping for. However, you can use the readings I have presented as a guide to what is possible. My hope is that you will be encouraged to "have a go" and create readings and retellings of your own. (I would love to see them! And if you want to share them with others, please do send them to my website – www.nonstopstoryshop.com – and we can pass them around.) In fact, the entire book is open to your constant revision. Feel free to adjust and adapt the readings to your needs. I have tried to be reasonably comprehensive in setting out the suggestions, but I haven't covered every base, so please do tinker and play!

Speaking of playing, it might be helpful to create a small group of "players" to do this, week by week. Many of us are accustomed to having a Worship Team to prepare and lead our sung worship. Why not another team to prepare and present these readings? They don't need to be "players" in the strictest sense of the word (although dramatic gifts would be helpful for many of the readings), but people who are keen to spend time with these texts, play with them a little, and give their creative energy to sharing them with the congregation.

I wonder if you have come across a charity called Open the Book? This is a rapidly growing group of volunteers who tell Bible stories to children in schools right across the UK, and I have been involved with them almost from the beginning. As this book is being written, Open the Book teams and individuals are in over a thousand schools and reaching something like a quarter of a million children every week. Having worked with many Open the Book groups, I am constantly told how excited the children are when they see the teams coming to their schools and know that they will be getting their Bible assembly! How amazing is that? The best assembly is the Bible assembly.

And how amazing would it be if, in our churches, week by week, when the time came for the Bible to be read, that there was a similar reaction among the congregation. Not that moment of switching off. Not that dry monotone. Not that fumbling over ancient names. Not that puzzled expression. Not that bored "been-there-done-that-heard-that-one-before", but a genuine sense of excitement because we are all about to encounter God's Word. We are all about to experience it. To taste it. To savour it.

That's my hope for this book.

Enjoy!

ADVENT

THE FIRST SUNDAY OF ADVENT

First reading

Isaiah 2:1–5

This short reading works well with some participation from the congregation. Everyone needs to be able to see a copy of the text (I'll be using the NIV) in printed, projected or electronic form. I prefer the text projected onto a screen as it ensures people are looking up and don't miss any direction from the front. Before starting the reading, the leader needs to explain, demonstrate, and practise the actions (see below) which correspond to six phrases from verses 3 and 4.

Leader: Reads verses 1 and 2. *(During verse 2 she holds her arms in the shape of a triangle, to represent the mountain.)*

Leader: Reads verses 3 and 4 *(at appropriate moment, doing the actions below which the congregation follow).*

"Come let us go…" *(echo the leader's earlier mountain action).*
"He will teach…" *(walking action).*
"The law will go out…" *(put one hand by mouth and move away from face).*
"He will judge…" *(bang imaginary gavel).*
"They will beat…" *(draw pretend sword from side, then hammer on it).*
"Nation will not take up…" *(draw sword again and fling it away).*

Leader: Reads verse 5 *(stretch out arms in a welcoming gesture).*

Everyone together: Repeat verse 5 three times, getting louder each time and building to a crescendo.

Gospel

. . . .

Matthew 24:36–44

This reading includes some actions and sounds that only the leader makes, but to involve the congregation get them to go *"whoosh"* with you. For a bit more participation you might also like everyone to join in with actions for the three key words in the "almost" chorus: *rain*: falling finger motion; *grain*: rub fingers together, as if letting grain fall through fingers; *ill-gotten gain*: with a couple of fingers pretend to pick someone's pocket.

"The coming of the Son of Man?" said Jesus. "Nobody knows the hour. Nobody knows the day. Not the angels. Not the Son. Only the Father, and he's not telling."
It's like rain and grain and ill-gotten gain.

Think of the days of Noah.
People were eating *(eating action)*,
People were drinking *(drinking action)*,
People were getting married *(holding flowers action)*,
Life went on as normal.
And then – *whoosh!* – the rains came *(rain sound)*,
And then – *whoosh!* – the floods followed *(waving motion with arms)*,
And then – *whoosh!* – they were washed away.
That's what the coming of the Son of Man will be like.
Like rain and grain and ill-gotten gain.

So think of the farmers.
Two of them will be in the field, and – *whoosh!* – one of them will be taken.
Two women will be grinding grain and – *whoosh!* – only one will be left.
Rain, grain and ill–gotten gain.

So, finally, think of the thief.
If the man who owned the burgled house had known the thief was coming, coming – *whoosh!* – to whisk away his stuff, he would have stayed awake and watched.
And you need to watch, as well, to be ready, because like that thief, the Son of Man will come at the time you least expect him.
Like rain and grain and ill-gotten gain.

THE SECOND SUNDAY OF ADVENT

First reading
....

Isaiah 11:1–10

This reading should work well if you have a fairly traditional congregation – one that is not accustomed to doing actions alongside Bible readings! The passage is full of powerful images that I think should be emphasized and acted out and the simple actions below can all be done quite seriously and gracefully to make a really beautiful and meaningful reading. In each verse, the reader puts an action to a word (or words), and then leads the congregation in repeating both the word and action.

However, if your congregation has lots of children and people who are accustomed to acting along, you might prefer the really active alternative version that follows.

Reader: Reads verse 1: "fruit" *(pluck apple from tree)*

Reader: Reads verse 2: "understanding" *(points to head or temple)* "power" *(flex muscles)*

Reader: Reads verse 3: "eyes" *(point to eyes)* "ears" *(point to ears)*

Reader: Reads verse 4: "needy" *(reach out hands, as if giving something away)* "mouth" *(point to mouth)*

Verse 5: "belt" *(pull pretend belt around waist)*

Verse 6: "lamb" *(pretend to hide innocent lamb in arms)* "together" *(interlock fingers)*

Verse 7: "together" *(repeat previous motion)*

Verse 8: "cobra" *(arm twisting upwards, weaving like a snake)*

Verse 9: "mountain" *(arms in triangle shape above head)* "sea" *(make wave-like motion with hands)*

Verse 10: "glorious" *(hands raised in praise)*.

Alternative "caffeinated" version

....

Isaiah 11:1–10

This version of the reading has a lot more actions and a bit of fun. You will need to teach the actions before you do the reading and the congregation won't remember them all. That's why you (and maybe another helper or two) will do the action the first time you say the word, then lead them in the action as you all say it together. Everyone needs to be able to see the text, ideally projected at the front, with the action words in bold type. So here are the verses, the words and the actions for this version. And, as is always the case with these readings, feel free to substitute actions that you think will work better with your church.

Some thoughts: you could also do this as a reading with lots of readers, each with an action or two. And it would make an amazing pageant-y sort of thing as well. A very different kind of Christmas pageant – with kids dressed up like sheep and goats and wolves and vipers. What a great way to celebrate God's Big Dream for his world and this incredible vision of his coming.

Verse 1: "shoot" *(thrust one arm in the air, like a shoot bursting out of the ground or, in this case, a stump)*
"stump" *(kneel down in a stumpy shape)*
"roots" *(reach out both hands, fingers apart, to look like roots)*
"fruit" *(pluck apple from tree)*

Verse 2: "wisdom" *(point to one side of head or temple with finger)*
"understanding" *(point to the other side of your head)*
"counsel" *(point finger as if giving direction)*
"power" *(muscle man pose)*
"knowledge" *(point to head again)*
"fear of the Lord" *(hands in front of face/shrinking away – think of Isaiah and his calling)*

Verse 3: "judge" *(bang pretend gavel)*
"eyes" *(point to eyes)*
"decide" *(finger on chin as if thinking)*
"ears" *(point to ears)*

Verse 4: "righteousness" *(hand on heart)*
"needy" *(reach out hands, as if giving something away)*
"justice" *(move hands up and down like scales)*
"poor" *(head down, look sad)*
"strike" *(striking motion)*
"mouth" *(point to mouth)*
"breath" *(blow)*
"wicked" *(make evil face and maybe evil laugh)*

Verse 5: "righteousness" *(hand on heart again)*
"belt" *(buckle belt)*
"faithfulness" *(hands clasped on heart)*
"waist" *(pretend to pull sash around waist)*

Verse 6: "wolf" *(howl)*
"lamb" *(baa)*
"leopard" *(little growl)*
"goat" *(naa)*
"calf" *(little moo)*
"lion" *(big roar)*
"together" *(hands clasped)*
"little child" *(say "hi" in tiny voice)*

Verse 7: "cow" *(big moo)*
"bear" *(arms in air, growl)*
"together" *(hands clasped again)*
"lion" *(big roar again)*
"ox" *(huge mooo!)*

Verse 8: "infant" *(waahhh)*
"cobra" *(hissssss)*
"young child" *(repeat little child)*
"nest" *(pretend to pull out baby snake and dangle!)*

Verse 9: "harm" *(ouch)*
"destroy" *(bigger ouch!)*
"mountain" *(make triangle shape with arms)*
"earth" *(make circle with hands)*
"knowledge" *(point to head)*
"sea" *(wavy motion with hands)*

Verse 10: "banner" (wave pretend banner)
"glorious" *(both arms raised in air)*.

Gospel
....

Matthew 3:1–12

I thought it might be nice to have some visual symbols to help us work our way through this story. They could be laid at the front on a table by the reader (perhaps a different reader for each section) or by a helper – a child, perhaps, or several children.

The story begins with a desert.
(Place a jar of sand on the table – maybe even one of those multicoloured/ layered jars of sand – whatever you've got!)

That's where John the Baptist is preaching. And what's his message?
    "Repent. The kingdom of heaven is near, here, close at hand. So close you can almost touch it."

His appearance is not by accident. It is the fulfilment of the prophecy that came through Isaiah.

"A voice. Someone calling in the desert. Prepare a way for the Lord. Make a straight path for him."

Next, there is honey.
(Place a jar of honey or a honeycomb on the table.)

That's what he eats. Well, that and locusts, but Sainsbury's was fresh out of those.

He wears camelskin clothes and a leather belt, and he's quite an attraction. People come from Jerusalem, and the rest of Judea, to see him.

And when they hear what he has to say, they admit that they are sinners, not fit for the kingdom.

So there is water.
(Put a jug of water on the table.)

And he baptises them in the Jordan River.

And then the snakes show up.
(Place a big rubber snake on the table.)

Well, they're the Pharisees and the Sadducees, actually. But "snakes" is what he calls them. Poisonous snakes, to be precise. Vipers.

And the rest of what he says to them doesn't get any nicer.

"Who warned you to flee from the coming wrath?" he asks.
"Don't act like being the children of Abraham will make any difference.
"God can make children of Abraham out of the stones you're standing on.
"No, fruit is what God wants. Good fruit. Fruit that proves you have changed your ways.
"Because trees that don't produce fruit get chopped down and thrown into the fire."

And speaking of fire…
(Place candle on the table.)

"There's someone coming after me," says John.
"Me. I baptise with water. As a sign of repentance.
"But him? He's more powerful than I'll ever be. I'm not fit to carry his sandals. And, yeah, he'll baptise, too. With the Holy Spirit. And with fire!
"That's right, he's got a winnowing fork and he knows how to use it. He's going to clear the threshing floor. He's going to gather the wheat. And he's going to burn up the chaff in his fire. A fire that no one will be able to quench."

THE THIRD SUNDAY OF ADVENT

Canticle: Magnificat

Luke 1:46b–55

Mighty One, Holy One, merciful forever.
Age to age, each generation spent.
Faithful One, Patient One, whose love cannot be severed.
There's no other word for him: Magnificent.

My soul cries out, my spirit sings
In praise of God, my Saviour,
Who looks at me and sees me as I am,
Then lifts me up on angel wings;
Hands that never waver,
And makes me part of his eternal plan.

Mighty One, Holy One, merciful forever.
Age to age, each generation spent.
Faithful One, Patient One, whose love cannot be severed.
There's no other word for him: Magnificent.

He shakes the proud and breaks the crown
And makes the strong man stumble.
He sets the rich man begging in the street,
Then reaches down and from the ground
Lifts up the poor and humble
And welcomes them to his forever feast.

Mighty One, Holy One, merciful forever.
Age to age, each generation spent.
Faithful One, Patient One, whose love cannot be severed.
There's no other word for him: Magnificent.

Gospel
....

Matthew 11:2–11

So John is in prison, and he hears what Jesus has been doing, and he starts to wonder, "Is this the way things are supposed to be when the Messiah comes?"

And the question under the question must surely be something like: "Why is the Messiah's prophet still sitting in the slammer?"

So he sends one of his own disciples to ask Jesus, "Are you really the one? Or should we be looking for someone else?"

It's a long way from what he said when he spotted Jesus by the Jordan: "Behold the lamb of God who takes away the sin of the world" – but then an extended stay in prison will do that to you.

So Jesus sends an answer back. And the answer is an unqualified, "Yes.

"The blind see. I am the one.

The lame walk. I am the one.

Lepers are healed. I am the one.

The deaf hear. I am the one.

The dead live. I am the one.

Good news is preached to the poor. I am the one."

And then Jesus says something else:

"Blessed is the man who does not fall away on account of me."

And the statement under that statement must surely be something like: "I know this doesn't look exactly like what you expected. But it's how I see the Messiah thing playing out. So trust me."

And in case that sounds a little harsh, Jesus makes sure that everyone knows how much respect he has for his cousin. Particularly (and in spite of his question) for his commitment.

"What did you think you'd find when you went to the desert to see John?" he asks the crowd. "A weak, uncertain man, blown like a reed in the wind? A pampered man, interested only in his own comfort? No, you went to see a prophet, and that's exactly what he is – born to prepare the way for God's Messiah.

"So let me make this clear – no man born of a woman is greater than John the Baptist."

And then he adds, "Yet he who is least in the kingdom of heaven is even greater than he."

And the statement under that statement must surely be something like: "In spite of his doubts, John has helped to usher in something new, something better, than the world has ever seen."

THE FOURTH SUNDAY OF ADVENT

Psalm
....

Psalm 80:1–7, 17–19

This psalm works really well if read responsively. There is an increasingly heightened emphasis on the nature of God by the simple addition of one word each time in verses 3, 7, and 19. Is it there because of an increasing sense of God's power and majesty, as the psalm progresses, or is it a reflection of the increasing desperation of the psalmist and the people he represents? Whatever the case, it's worth pointing this out, both so that the congregation doesn't just say the same thing each time, and to help them get a better sense of the psalm itself.

If you are interested in adding actions, I would keep them simple. Everyone could raise their hands in the air for the response verses, more in pleading than in praise. Some optional actions for the leader are listed below.

Leader: Reads verses 1–2 *(two hands spread apart for "enthroned between the cherubim line).*

Congregation: Reads verse 3.

Leader: Reads verses 4–6 *(a finger running down the cheek for the "tears" line).*

Congregation: Reads verse 7.

Leader: Reads verses 17–18 *(right hand reaching out and resting on a pretend shoulder for the "let your hand rest" line).*

Congregation: Reads verse 19.

Gospel
....

Matthew 1:18, 21–25

This is how the birth of Jesus Christ came about.
    With a betrayal. Or so it seemed to Joseph.

He was pledged to be married to Mary. And then he discovered she was pregnant. And he knew the baby wasn't his.

This is how the birth of Jesus Christ came about.

With an act of compassion. An act of love.

He could have disgraced her publicly. He could have let everyone know what she'd done. He could have punished her and shamed her. He could have destroyed her. But he didn't.

He decided, instead, to bring an end to the relationship, quietly.

This is how the birth of Jesus Christ came about.

With a divine message.

An angel appeared to Joseph and explained to him that the baby Mary carried had been conceived through the Holy Spirit. And that wasn't all. Mary would give birth to a son and he would be called Jesus – the One come to save his people from their sins.

This is how the birth of Jesus Christ came about.

With a promise.

A promise made by a prophet hundreds of years before Joseph was born. A promise about a virgin giving birth to a boy called Immanuel. And the promise in the boy's name – God with us.

This is how the birth of Jesus Christ came about.

With a reconciliation.

Joseph took Mary as his wife. He had no union with her until she gave birth. And when she did, he gave the boy the name the angel had told him. Another name of promise. Jesus.

This is how the birth of Jesus Christ came about.

With a betrayal, an act of love, a divine message, a promise, and a reconciliation.

When you think about it, you could say the same about his death.

CHRISTMAS EVE

First Reading

2 Samuel 7:1–5, 8–11, 16

When King David was finally settled in his palace, he had a little chat with Nathan the prophet.

"Look at this place I live in. Cedar walls. Cedar doors. Cedar floors. It's amazing!

"Now take a look at God's place – the place where the Ark of the Covenant sits. It's a tent. Just a tent. And not even a new tent."

Nathan saw where the king was going. David had a nice house, and he wanted to make God a nice house, too. Fair enough. So Nathan told David, "Whatever you have in mind, go ahead and do it, for the Lord is with you."

But God had a different idea. And that very night he passed it on to Nathan:

"David wants to build a house for me? I'm not sure he's the one to do it. But I would definitely like to build a house for HIM.

"Tell him that I have already laid the foundations. I took him from the fields and from the flocks and made him the ruler of my people.

"Tell him the walls are up, too. I have been with him and protected him from all his enemies.

"And as for splendour and the quality of the building materials, tell him that his house will rank among the greatest on the earth.

"In fact, tell him that his house will be more like a city – a place for all my people to dwell, with strong gates to keep their enemies out and soft beds so David can get some rest at last.

"And finally, tell him that the house I want to build for him will not crumble or rot or tumble down. Tell King David that I want to build him a house – a house that will stand forever."

Second Reading

Acts 13:16–26

There's a story behind the story, a reason why we're here tonight, that started long before an expectant mother and her husband found lodgings in the town of Bethlehem.

It's a story for everyone – Jew and Gentile alike.

It's a story about choice – how God chose his people Israel.

It's a story about care – how God took them to Egypt to save them from famine and prosper them.

It's a story about deliverance – how God led them out of slavery to freedom.

It's a story about patience – how God endured the conduct of his people in the wilderness for forty years.

It's a story about inheritance – how God gave his people a land to call their own.

It's a story about a nation – ruled by judges and then by kings.

It's a story about one of those kings in particular – David, a man after God's own heart.

And it's a story about one of David's descendants – Jesus, the saviour – promised to Israel and heralded by John the Baptist.

God's choosing and care and deliverance and patience and inheritance and promise and rule: this is God's story of salvation. It started a long time ago. It's been going for thousands of years.

And tonight the story is for *us*.

CHRISTMAS

CHRISTMAS DAY

First reading

Isaiah 9:2–7

The point of this reading is to break it up in a way that draws attention to its meaning. So you will need a leader and two groups in the church. You may find it helpful to have someone leading each of those groups as well. Everyone needs to be able to see the text, ideally on a screen, and colour coding the different groups will also be helpful (just make sure the colours you choose make the text easy to read).

Leader: The people walking in darkness

Group 1: Have seen a great light;

Leader: On those living in the land of deep darkness

Group 2: A light has dawned.

Leader: You have enlarged the nation
and increased their joy;
they rejoice before you

Group 1: As people rejoice at the harvest,

Group 2: As warriors rejoice
when dividing the plunder.

Leader: For as in the day of Midian's defeat,
you have shattered
the yoke that burdens them,

Group 1: The bar across their shoulders,

Group 2: The rod of their oppressor.

Leader: Every warrior's boot used in battle
and every garment rolled in blood

Group 1: Will be destined for burning,

Group 2: Will be fuel for the fire.

All: For to us a child is born,
to us a son is given,
and the government will be on his shoulders.

And he will be called
Wonderful Counsellor, Mighty God,
Everlasting Father, Prince of Peace.

Leader: Of the increase of his government and peace
there will be no end.

Group 1: He will reign on David's throne
and over his kingdom,

Group 2: Establishing and upholding it
with justice and righteousness
from that time on and for ever.

All: The zeal of the Lord Almighty
will accomplish this.

Gospel

Luke 2:1–14 [15–20]

Once there was a king.

A king who ruled his own people, and the people his people had conquered.

One day the king decided to count his people. To show how powerful he was, maybe. Or maybe it was so that he could rule his people and control his people more effectively.

In any case, the word went out to his people, and everyone in the kingdom had to return to the place their family had come from, to be counted.

One of those people was a man named Joseph.

The king had never met this man. He didn't even know he existed. He was just a number – or soon would be: a number on a list of the people to be counted in one of his conquered lands.

Joseph was engaged to be married to a girl called Mary, someone else the king had never heard of. Another number. Another list.

And Mary was expecting a baby. Not yet a number at all.

So Joseph and Mary travelled from Nazareth, the place where they lived, to Bethlehem, the place where Joseph's family had come from. It was a long journey – ninety miles or so. And not a particularly convenient journey given Mary's condition. But kings don't think about those kinds of things. They just expect their people to do what they're told.

So that's what Joseph did. And because Bethlehem was crowded with many other people doing what they were told, there were no rooms at the inn. So they found a place to stay in a stable. And it was there that Mary gave birth to her child – a son. And because they were in a stable, Mary wrapped her baby up in cloths and laid him in a manger: another tiny number for the king's list.

In the fields surrounding Bethlehem, there were yet more people. And even less important ones. Shepherds, watching their sheep. We don't even know their names. And you can be certain the first king didn't. Just more numbers.

But there was another king who did. Who knew their names and their ages and even the number of hairs on their heads. That was a different kind of counting all together. And that's because he was a different kind of king.

The King of Heaven, as it happens. So it will come as no surprise that, when he wanted to talk with these shepherds, the heavens opened and an angel appeared.

The shepherds were terrified. Who wouldn't be? So the angel told them not to be afraid. The angel explained to them that he had come with good news. The angel assured them that the news would bring them joy. And that this joy would touch everyone.

And then the angel told them where to find that joy.

In a manger. In a stable. In Bethlehem.

That's right. The baby who had just been born, the baby of the mother who the first king had never heard of, was the Son of the King of Heaven himself – the long-awaited saviour the King of Heaven had been promising to send to his people for years.

So the angel called for his angel friends and they celebrated the baby's birth and sang praises to the King of Heaven.

And when they had gone, the shepherds whom the first king had never heard of went to see the baby and the man and the woman he'd never heard of either.

And when they had seen the baby, they wandered through the streets of Bethlehem, telling everyone what had happened, telling everyone what they had seen.

And while the counting went on, up and down and all around the kingdom, the person who counted the most was born tiny and obscure. And a new story was born, as well. A story that would change the world.

Once there was a king…

THE FIRST SUNDAY OF CHRISTMAS

Psalm
. . . .

Psalm 148

This is a call-and-response treatment of the psalm, which will save teaching the congregation too many actions. The leader (A) does her own set of actions with her lines. The congregation (B) follows with their own actions and should probably have a leader of their own. It will be best if you teach the congregation their actions before you begin and explain that the leader will be doing a different set of actions. Fortunately, each verse, apart from the first and the last, breaks up nicely into A and B parts, so I will just list the verse and the actions (mostly).

Everyone says: "Praise the Lord" *(in an enthusiastic manner!)*

Verse 1: A *(Point to the heavens.)*
B *(All raise up both arms to the heavens.)*

Verse 2: A *(Draws halo round head.)*
B *(All flap angel wings.)*

Verse 3: A *(Draws circle in air for sun, crescent for moon.)*
B *(All do a "twinkle twinkle" action with the hands.)*

Verse 4: A *(Repeat action from verse 1 but jump up as you do it.)*
B *(All raise hands in air and make flowing, watery movement)*

Verses 5–6: Leader reads these verses alone and with no actions *(everyone else gets a rest!)*

Verse 7: A *(Point down to the earth – or stamp foot.)*
B *(All wave arms like an octopus.)*

Verse 8: A *(Move hands up and down, like rainstorm.)*
B *(All wave hands from side to side like wind in a storm.)*

Verse 9: A *(Make triangular mountain shape with arms.)*
B *(Make shape of tree with body straight and arms stretched out like branches.)*

Verse 10: A *(Roar – hands out like claws – and moo – fingers to head like horns.)*
B *(Make insect noises – fingers like antennae to head – and bird noises – flap arm wings.)*

Verse 11: A *(Stretch forth hand as if giving an order.)*
B *(All pretend to put crown on head.)*

Verse 12: A *(Show muscles and pretend to brush or stroke hair.)*
B *(All stoop over and hold walking stick then jump about in a childlike fashion.)*

Verses 13–14: Leader reads these verse on her own.

Everyone shouts: "Praise the Lord."

Gospel
....

Matthew 2:13–23

After the leader has said the words "And so the prophet's words came true", it might be nice for the congregation to repeat the line throughout.

And so the prophet's words came true:
 Once the Magi had gone, Joseph had a dream. The angel of the Lord appeared to him and told him to take Mary and Jesus to Egypt, for King Herod intended to find the baby and kill him.
 And that's what Joseph did, right there, in the middle of the night. And they stayed there, until Herod was dead.

And so the prophet's words came true:
 "Out of Egypt I called my son."

Herod was furious when he learned that the Magi had left without telling him the whereabouts of the child. So he did what, to his mind, was the next best thing, or maybe the next worst thing! Using the time frame of their journey, he calculated that the child would be no older than two. And then he commanded that all boys in Bethlehem, two years old and under, should be taken from their parents and killed.

And so the prophet's words came true:

"Hear a voice from Ramah –
Hear weeping and mourning,
Hear Rachel weeping for her children,
Hear weeping beyond comfort
Because her children are no more."

Once Herod had died, Joseph had a dream. It was the angel of the Lord, who told him that it was now safe to take Mary and Jesus back to Israel.

So that's what Joseph did. But when he heard that Herod's son, Archelaus, was now in charge of Judea he was afraid to go there. So, guided by yet one more dream, he took Mary and Jesus to Nazareth, up north, in Galilee.

And so the prophet's words came true:
"He will be called a Nazarene."

THE SECOND SUNDAY OF CHRISTMAS

Second reading

Ephesians 1:3–14

The thing about some of Paul's letters is that there is so much going on, and so much important teaching being shared, that they can be really hard to follow. But they *are* letters, and it struck me that their recipients might well have come up with some questions and responses, perhaps like those I've added below. (They definitely occurred to me as I read this letter.) I hope that this reading makes this extract from Paul's letter easier to understand. I would use a second reader or the congregation to respond to reader 1.

Reader 1: Reads verse 3.

Reader 2/Congregation: Every spiritual blessing? Wow, that's amazing! When did this happen?

Reader 1: Reads verse 4, ending with "sight".

Reader 2/Congregation: Before the creation of the world? As long ago as that?

Reader 1: Reads verse 4 from "In love" to end of verse 5.

Reader 2/Congregation: So he's loved us forever then? And to what end?

Reader 1: Reads verse 6.

Reader 2/Congregation: So what does that mean for us – specifically?

Reader 1: Reads verses 7 and 8.

Reader 2/Congregation: Forgiveness of sins? The riches of God's grace lavished* on us? Anything else? [*I LOVE THAT WORD!]

Reader 1: Reads verses 9 and 10.

Reader 2/Congregation: So it's not just us he's concerned for, then? His grace extends to everyone and everything. And, remind me again – what's this for?

Reader 1: Reads verses 11 and 12.

Reader 2/Congregation: The praise of his glory. There's that phrase again. Anything else?

Reader 1: Reads "And you…" from verse 13.

Reader 2/Congregation: Hang on, are you talking to us, now? I thought we already were the "us". Why are you saying "And you"? Wait a minute – it's that Jew/Gentile thing, isn't it? God's plan started with Jews like you, Paul, and now it extends to Gentiles like us in Ephesus! Carry on…

Reader 1: Reads rest of verses 13 and 14.

Reader 2/Congregation: So we're in, too! All of us. Saved by Christ and marked by his Spirit – until the day he accomplishes everything he has planned forever.
To the praise of his glory!

Gospel

John 1:[1–9] 10–18

Giving the congregation a simple line to say will help them concentrate on this familiar passage. Most of the text is read by the leader who will indicate when they say their line – "Tell us about The Word!"

An alternative approach would be to use the original Bible text and simply insert the "Tell us about The Word!" lines in the corresponding places.

Tell us about The Word!
He was there in the beginning.

Tell us about The Word!
He was with God.

Tell us about The Word!
He WAS God and (I know it's hard to get your head around this) he was WITH God in the beginning.

Tell us about The Word!
Everything – absolutely everything that exists – was made through him.

Tell us about The Word!
Life is in him – and that life is the light for everyone.

Tell us about The Word!
That light shines in the darkness – but the darkness doesn't understand it.

Tell us about The Word!
Why don't I let someone else do it? A man sent from God. A man named John. He wasn't the light himself. He just came to tell people about it – as a kind of witness – so that people would believe that the true light was really coming into the world.

Tell us about The Word!
The Word was in the world, but even though the world was made through him, the world didn't recognize him for who he was. It was like he was a stranger in the house that he had built.

Tell us about The Word!
Some people did recognize him and receive him and believe in him. And he gave those people the right to become children of God. Children born, not naturally, by the decision and action of human parents but born of God.

Tell us about The Word!
Having said that, The Word himself, was born of human flesh and lived among us. And we were witnesses to his glory – the glory of this Unique One who came from the Father, filled with grace and truth.

Tell us about The Word!
John the Baptist said it best: "The one who comes after me is even better than me – because he was before me"

Tell us about The Word!
We have all been blessed – blessed again and again – by his overflowing grace. Moses gave us the law, yes. But grace? Grace and truth? They came to us through Jesus Christ.

Tell us about The Word!
No one has ever seen God. But this God, the Unique One who sits (and I know this is hard to get your head around) at the Father's side – this Unique One has made God known to us.

EPIPHANY

THE EPIPHANY

First reading

Isaiah 60:1–6

I'm a great fan of processions – and this reading really lends itself to one of those! The passage is about the nations' response to what God is doing for his people. What he is doing is announced joyfully in the first part of the passage, and then God's people are called to lift up their eyes and see the crowd of people coming their way. You need a crowd – maybe volunteers can be self-selecting to take part in the procession below and someone to lead the reading.

The procession begins at verse 4b (below). Participants can parade down a centre aisle, or come from the sides, or from behind the leader – whatever works in your building. Ideally, one of them, or all of them together, should shout out the verses that accompany their appearing. But if that's too much, then let the leader read those verses and just let those in the procession walk.

> **Leader** (addressing verses to congregation with emphasis on final
> sentence): *"Arise shine, for your light has come,*
> *and the glory of the Lord rises upon you.*
> *See, darkness covers the earth*
> *and thick darkness is over the peoples,*
> *but the Lord rises upon you*
> *and his glory appears over you.*
> *Nations will come to your light,*
> *and kings to the brightness of your dawn.*
> *Lift up your eyes and look about you:*
> (The procession begins.)

Leader: *All assemble and come to you;*
your sons come from afar,
and your daughters are carried on the hip.
Then you will look and be radiant,
your heart will throb and swell with joy;
(Men and women, boys and girls, process arm in arm.)

Leader: *The wealth on the seas will be brought to you,*
to you the riches of the nations will come.
(Wealth on the seas: could have people carrying stuffed toy fish, fishing equipment, treasure chests. "AARRRR." Riches of the nations: people carry anything that signifies wealth – except for gold, which will come later!)

Leader: *Herds of camels will cover your land,*
young camels of Midian and Ephah.
(Camels are tricky. People carrying pictures of camels, plush camel, or even a camel puppet.)

Leader: *And all from Sheba will come,*
bearing gold and incense
and proclaiming the praise of the Lord.
(People carrying gold and ornate jars for incense.)

Second reading

Ephesians 3:1–12

This reading works in the same way as the one from Ephesians in the previous section, except that there is a lot less for the congregation to say. In fact, it's just one line: "Tell us about this mystery, Paul."

Again, I think that breaking the passage up this way helps to remind the congregation that it's a letter, helps them to focus on the point that Paul is making, and gives them the chance to focus on smaller bites of text at a time.

Leader: Reads verses 1–3.

Congregation: Tell us about this mystery, Paul.

Leader: Reads verses 4–5.

Congregation: Tell us about this mystery, Paul.

Leader: Reads verse 6 (with great emphasis, because this IS the mystery!)

Congregation: Tell us about this mystery, Paul.

Leader: Reads verses 7–9.

Congregation: Tell us about this mystery, Paul.

Leader: Reads verses 10–12.

THE FIRST SUNDAY OF EPIPHANY – THE BAPTISM OF CHRIST

Psalm

....

Psalm 29

This is a reading that needs to be shouted rather than read, because it's all about the power of the voice of the Lord! So you will need a main reader/ leader to begin and finish the reading. And, ideally, you will need to divide the congregation into two groups. This will give each group a break from shouting and also provide some variety in the experience.

Make it clear, from the start, that they need to be loud, but also need to enjoy and appreciate the meaning of the verses they are reading. It will help if you have the verses on a screen at the front, with the words for each groups in a different colour.

Leader: Reads verses 1–2.

Group 1: Reads verse 3.

Group 2: Reads verse 4.

Group 1: Reads verse 5.

Group 2: Reads verse 6.

Group 1: Reads verse 7.

Group 2: Reads verse 8.

Leader: Reads verse 9. And everyone shouts "Glory!" together.

Leader: Reads verses 10–11 *(starting this section loudly and getting quieter and quieter as he gets to "the Lord blesses his people with peace").*

Gospel
....

Matthew 3:13–17

You need two readers for this. One says the words in capitals and leads the congregation as they repeat them. The other reader reads the rest of the text. At the end, everyone says all the words in capitals together.

Reader 1: When the time came for Jesus to be baptised, he travelled from Galilee to the Jordan River to be baptised by his cousin John.

Reader 2/Congregation: JOHN IS NOT KEEN.

Reader 1: But John was not keen on the idea. "I need to be baptised by YOU," he said. "Not the other way round."

Reader 2/Congregation: JESUS INSISTS.

Reader 1: "No," said Jesus. "We need to do it this way. It's one of the good things that God wants me to do."

Reader 2/Congregation: JOHN GIVES IN.

Reader 1: So John gave in. He baptised Jesus.

Reader 2/Congregation: GOD SHOWS UP.

Reader 1: And as Jesus came up out of the water, he saw heaven open up. He saw God's Spirit coming down from heaven like a dove and landing on him.

Reader 2/Congregation: AND HE IS PLEASED.

All together: JESUS WANTS TO BE BAPTISED. JOHN IS NOT KEEN. JESUS INSISTS. JOHN GIVES IN. GOD SHOWS UP. AND HE IS PLEASED.

Reader 1: And he heard the voice of God saying, "This is my Son. I love him. And I am very pleased with him."

THE SECOND SUNDAY OF EPIPHANY

First reading

Isaiah 49:1–7

Before starting this reading you might want to begin by explaining that this is a conversation between the Lord and his servant. So you need two readers, one for each of these roles. I think this approach will help to break up the reading and also help the congregation to better understand what it's about.

> **The Servant:** *Listen to me, you islands;*
> *hear this, you distant nations:*
> *Before I was born the Lord called me;*
> *from my mother's womb he has spoken my name.*
> *He made my mouth like a sharpened sword,*
> *in the shadow of his hand he hid me;*
> *he made me into a polished arrow*
> *and concealed me in his quiver.*
> *He said to me,*
>
> **The Lord:** *"You are my servant,*
> *Israel, in whom I will display my splendour."*
>
> **The Servant:** *But I said, "I have laboured in vain;*
> *I have spent my strength for nothing at all.*
> *Yet what is due me is in the Lord's hand,*
> *And my reward is with my God."*
>
> *And now the Lord says –*
>
> *He who formed me in the womb to be his servant*
> *to bring Jacob back to him*
> *and gather Israel to himself,*
> *for I am honoured in the eyes of the Lord*
> *and my God has been my strength –*

he says:

The Lord: *"It is too small a thing for you to be my servant*
to restore the tribes of Jacob
and bring back those of Israel I have kept.
I will also make you a light for the Gentiles,
that my salvation may reach to the ends of the earth."

The Servant: *This is what the Lord says –*
the Redeemer and Holy One of Israel –
to him who was despised and abhorred by the nation,
to the servant of rulers:

The Lord: *"Kings will see you and stand up,*
princes will see you and stand up,
because of the Lord, who is faithful,
the Holy One of Israel, who has chosen you."

Psalm

. . . .

Psalm 40:1–11

Apparently this psalm was the inspiration for the U2 song "40", which you can find on their album "War". They adapt the psalm to form their chorus, but we're going to say the part of verse three from which it was adapted.

Start by teaching the chorus – "He put a new song in my mouth. A hymn of praise to our God" – to the congregation. Then lead them in the chorus after the leader reads the verses below. An alternative option would be to use a different reader for each section.

Leader: Reads verses 1–3.

Congregation: *Says chorus:*
"He put a new song in my mouth
A hymn of praise to our God"

Leader: Reads verses 4–5.

Congregation: *Says chorus.*

Leader: Reads verses 6–8.

Congregation: *Says chorus.*

Leader: Reads verses 9–10.

Congregation: *Says chorus.*

Leader: Reads verse 11.

Congregation: *Says chorus. (You might want to repeat the chorus to finish.)*

THE THIRD SUNDAY OF EPIPHANY

Second reading

1 Corinthians 1:10–18

Here's another treatment that attempts to make it clear that Paul's letters really were letters and that the original readers would have received them that way. And they would have responded to them – even if just "in their heads" – as they were reading or listening to them. You will need readers, one to read the text and another to read the comments, responses, and questions.

Reader 1: I appeal to you, brothers and sisters, in the name of our Lord Jesus Christ, that all of you agree with one another in what you say and that there may be no divisions among you, but that you be perfectly united in mind and thought.

Reader 2: "Why? What have you heard?"

Reader 1: My brothers and sisters, some from Chloe's household have informed me that there are quarrels among you.

Reader 2 *(with a sigh)***:** "Chloe's household again! Those people just can't keep their mouths shut. So what have they been telling you?"

Reader 1: What I mean is this: One of you says, "I follow Paul"; another, "I follow Apollos"; another, "I follow Cephas"; still another, "I follow Christ."

Reader 2 *(sheepishly)***:** "Yes… we-e-ll… ummm… there might be a little of that going on. It's only natural, when you get a diverse group of people together. But I'm with you, Paul. You can count on me!"

(Verse 13 gets chopped up a bit here.)

Reader 1: "Is Christ divided?"

Reader 2: "When you put it that way – no."

Reader 1: "Was Paul crucified for you?"

Reader 2: "Not exactly, no – that would be Christ, again."

Reader 1: "Were you baptised into the name of Paul?"

Reader 2: "Okay, okay – Jesus again. I've got it."

Reader 1: I thank God that I did not baptise any of you except Crispus and Gaius, so no one can say that you were baptised in my name.

Reader 2: "Well, there was the household of Stephanas –"

Reader 1 *(interrupting):* (Yes, I also baptised the household of Stephanas, beyond that, I don't remember if I baptised anyone else.)

Reader 2: "Don't think so, but then I did miss a couple weekends when I was on holiday."

Reader 1: For Christ did not send me to baptise, but to preach the gospel – not with wisdom and eloquence, lest the cross of Christ be emptied of its power. For the message of the cross is foolishness to those who are perishing, but to us who are being saved it is the power of God.

Reader 2: "Which is sort of the point, after all, isn't it? And again, it all comes back to Jesus. I think I've got it, Paul."

Gospel

Matthew 4:12–23

This is a sort of travelling story. So why not get out your Bible map or first-century GPS and follow each leg of the journey? You could have one reader, pausing briefly between each leg of the journey, or alternate between two readers.

Leg 1: Jesus hears that John the Baptist has been put in prison, so he leaves Judea and travels north to his home town, Nazareth, in Galilee.

Leg 2: He leaves Nazareth and goes to live in Capernaum, which is by the Sea of Galilee.

Leg 3: Capernaum is in the area of Zebulun and Naphtali. And Jesus' presence there fulfils a prophecy from the book of Isaiah – that in the land of Zebulun and Naphtali people walking in darkness will see a great light.

Leg 4: So Jesus starts to preach there – the dawning of the light – the kingdom of heaven is NEAR! (Even his message has to do with distance.)

Leg 5: Then he goes walking beside the sea – travelling again – and he comes across two brothers, fishermen, Peter and Andrew, casting their net into the lake. And what does he say to them?

Leg 6: "Come and follow me." More travelling! "And I will make you fishers of men." So they leave their nets and off they go – after Jesus.

Leg 7: They carry on, along the side of the sea, and they meet two more brothers, also fishermen, James and John, the sons of Zebedee. Jesus offers them the same invitation he'd offered Peter and Andrew. And they take off after Jesus, too – leaving their dad to untangle his nets.

Leg 8: And then what does Jesus do? Now that he's got a few followers, he just keeps on walking – through the whole of Galilee – teaching, preaching the good news of the kingdom, and healing sick people wherever he finds them.

Like I said – it's a travelling story.

THE FOURTH SUNDAY OF EPIPHANY

First reading

....

1 Kings 17:8–16

This story and the next will work best if you teach the actions and responses before the storytelling begins. This will get the congregation guessing about which story you are going to tell and reinforce the story along the way.

The story starts with a famine.
 A famine *(rub empty tummies – oooh)*.
 A famine in the whole of the land of Israel that reached even to their neighbours in the north. A famine sent by the Lord because King Ahab worshipped foreign gods.

The story continues with a widow.
 A widow *(look sad, awww)*.
 "Go to Zarephath," God told his prophet Elijah, "to a people who are not my people, and I will use a widow there to provide you with food."

And then there is a gate *(pretend to open gate – squeaky sound)*.
 So Elijah went to Zarephath, and at the gates of the town he found a widow gathering sticks. So he asked her for some water. And he asked for some bread.

And the answer he got was a "No" *(shake heads – no)*.
 "I don't have any bread," the widow said. "Just a little flour in a jar and a little oil in a jug. So I will take these sticks and make a fire and bake a little meal with what little I have left. And then my little boy and I will eat it – and lie down and die."

So Elijah makes a promise *(cross heart, say "a promise")*.
 "There's no need to be afraid," he said. "Go home. Make two cakes of bread out of what you have. One for me, and one for yourself. And you will have more than enough. For God himself has told me that your little jar of flour will not be used up and your little jug of oil will not run out until the rains return and the famine ends."

So the woman makes some bread *(pretend to mix ingredients in a bowl – clackety clackety clack – making stirring motion with a spoon, or make a kneading motion).*

And just as Elijah promised, the jar did not run out and the jug did not run dry and there was enough food for her and her son and the prophet until the rains returned.

And that's why the story finishes with a Wow! *(Everyone shouts "Wow!")*

Gospel

John 2:1–11

The story begins with a wedding. *(Pretend to hold bouquet like a bride and hum first line of "Here Comes the Bride".)*

It was a wedding at Cana in Galilee. And among the guests were Jesus, Jesus' mother, and his disciples.

The story continues with a shock. *(Hold hands to side of face, scream or inhale breath in a shocked manner.)*

The wine ran out. And Jesus' mother went to tell him so.

And then there is a question. *(Hold finger to chin with puzzled look.)*

"What do you want me to do?" asks Jesus. "It's not my time yet."

But his mum perseveres and tells the servants to do whatever he asks of them.

As it happens, there are six stone water jars nearby *(hold out arms in circle shape as if struggling to lift jars – with a grunt)*. Stone water jars used by the Jews for ceremonial washing. They each hold somewhere between twenty and thirty gallons.

So Jesus tells the servants to fill them with water.

And then there is quite a lot of pouring. *(Pretend to pour water into jars – making glug-glug-glug sounds.)*

And when the jars are full, he tells the servants to draw some out and take it to the man in charge of the banquet.

And when he tastes it, there is another shock. *(Pretend to taste it and then shout "Du vin! C'est magnifique!")*

So he goes to the bridegroom and praises him for saving the best wine for last.

And with the first of his many miracles, Jesus just saves the day. *(Everyone shouts "Hooray!")*

THE PRESENTATION OF CHRIST IN THE TEMPLE (CANDLEMAS)

Psalm
. . . .

Psalm 24:[1–6] 7–10

The questions in this psalm make it a perfect candidate for a call-and-response reading. In this case, I think that the congregation should ask the questions, and the reader should supply the answers. Again, I think it is helpful, if possible, for the words of the psalm to be projected at the front with clearly different text colours for the reader and the congregation.

Reader: Reads verses 1–2.

Congregation: Reads verse 3.

Reader: Reads verses 4–7.

Congregation: Reads the first line of verse 8, "Who is this King of Glory?"

Reader: Reads rest of verse 8 and verse 9.

Congregation: Reads the first line of verse 10.

Reader: Reads the rest of verse 10.

Gospel
. . . .

Luke 2:22–40

Only one reader is needed but they say each of the lines three times. In the first part of the couplet, this gives them the opportunity to emphasize different parts of the line and milk it of its meaning. In the second part, it gives everyone else the opportunity to "catch on" and really enjoy joining in the actions (below). The congregation need to be taught the actions before the reading begins.

Mary and Joseph went into Jerusalem
Carrying baby Jesus, whom they loved *(cradling – goo).*

They were there because the law required them to present him to the Lord –
Their firstborn as a gift to the Lord above *(look up – oooh!)*.

And so they made a sacrifice, just as the law required:
Two young pigeons, or a pair of doves *(flap wings – coo)*.

Now living in Jerusalem was a man called Simeon,
A righteous man, devout and true *(finger in air)*.

The Holy Spirit had told this man a most unusual thing;
He would see God's saviour before his life was through *(choke)*.

So, moved by that same spirit, he went to the temple grounds
And was there as Mary and Joseph came walking through *(fingers walk)*.

Simeon held the baby, and looking at the parents said,
"I've got an important message for you" *(point)*.

"God has let me see your baby, and I praise him for that now
Before I bid this mortal life adieu *(wave goodbye)*.

"For he is God's salvation, prepared for *all* to see,
For those who are and those who are not Jews" *(make star of David shape with finger)*.

Mary and Joseph were amazed by all that Simeon said
And secretly wanted to leap and shout "Wahoo!" *(shout "Wahoo!")*

Then Simeon blessed the family, and looking at Mary said,
"There's one thing left on which you need to chew *(make chewing motion)*.

"This child will be the making of many in this land
But some will fall and consider him taboo *(hold at arm's length)*.

"Whose heart's with God, whose heart is not – all will be revealed.
And, my dear, that sword will pass through your heart, too" *(sword stabbing motion as if through heart)*.

ORDINARY TIME

PROPER 1 – THE FIFTH SUNDAY BEFORE LENT

First Reading

Isaiah 58:1–9a[b–12]

This is such a powerful passage, full of such strong imagery, that there needs to be some way to bring it all to light. So here's my suggestion: one reader will be the voice of God and read most of the passage, and another reader will be the voice of Israel in verse 3.

The congregation will have something to look at during the reading as, I think, you will need two people to act out the pictures the passage evokes. If you have dancers in your church, they would be perfect. Or people who are good with flags. Actors would do – in fact anyone who can use their body to bring a picture to life.

Reader 1: Reads verses 1–2, with nothing going on behind.

Reader 2: Reads verse 3 – Israel's response, ending with "you have not noticed".

Reader 1: Reads rest of verse 3, and verses 4–12 – God's response. (Allow time for the actors to keep up.)

Throughout this part of the reading your two movement people appear behind, or at the reader's side – wherever they are best seen. And then they bring each verse to life as it is read. I have suggested some motions/actions below, but people who are accustomed to doing this will probably have better ideas!

Verse 3b: *One pretends to beat another.*

Verse 4: *They fight/wrestle each other.*

Verse 5: *They bow their heads and fall to their knees.*

Verse 6: *One pulls the other's arms apart, as if breaking chains. The other lifts yoke from the first one's shoulder.*

Verse 7: *They take turns feeding, sheltering (hands as roof over head) and clothing each other.*

Verse 8: *They pretend to watch the sun rise, then arms upraised, mouths open in awe at the beauty of it.*

Verse 9a: *They lift hands to mouth, head raised, as if calling.*

Verse 9b: *Again remove yoke and throw away, then point finger and slap it away.*

Verse 10: *One on knees, the other feeds then lifts up to feet – then they look at the rising dawn light again.*

Verse 11: *One takes the other's hand and leads in a short walk, then both are plants, growing, with arms up waving as branches.*

Verse 12: *Pretend to build a brick wall and then stand back and, with arms, gesture towards the rebuilt ruin, smiling.*

Psalm

....

Psalm 112:1–9 [10]

I think that the *meaning* of this psalm opens up with the asking of one simple question: "How are they blessed?" So I suggest that you have one reader to read the passage, and get the congregation to ask that question again and again, throughout. It's very simple, and may prompt each person to ask themselves that question, "How have I been blessed?" And if you think that the question pops up too often, you could always ask it between every other verse.

Reader: Reads verse 1.

Congregation: "Tell us, how are they blessed?"

Reader: Reads verse 2.

Congregation: "Tell us, how are they blessed?"

Reader: Reads verse 3.

Congregation: "Tell us, how are they blessed?"

Reader: Reads verse 4.

Congregation: "Tell us, how are they blessed?"

Reader: Reads verse 5.

Congregation: "Tell us, how are they blessed?"

Reader: Reads verse 6.

Congregation: "Tell us, how are they blessed?"

Reader: Reads verse 7.

Congregation: "Tell us, how are they blessed?"

Reader: Reads verse 8.

Congregation: "Tell us, how are they blessed?"

Reader: Reads verse 9.

Congregation: "Tell us, how are they blessed?"

Reader: Reads verse 10.

PROPER 2
– THE FOURTH SUNDAY BEFORE LENT

First Reading

Deuteronomy 30:15–20

Because this reading is all about stark contrasts between life and death and blessings and curses, I thought it would be helpful to have two readers to present those contrasts.

Reader 1: See, I set before you today life and prosperity,

Reader 2: Death and destruction.

Reader 1: For I command you today to love the Lord your God, to walk in obedience to his ways, and to keep his commands, decrees and laws; then you will live and increase, and the Lord your God will bless you in the land you are entering to possess.

Reader 2: But if your heart turns away and you are not obedient, and if you are drawn away to bow down to other gods and worship them, I declare to you this day that you will certainly be destroyed. You will not live long in the land you are crossing the Jordan to enter and possess.

Reader 1: This day I call heaven and earth as witnesses against you that I have set before you life and

Reader 2: Death.

Reader 1: Blessings and

Reader 2: Curses.

Reader 1: Now choose life, so that you and your children may live and that you may love the Lord your God, listen to his voice, and hold fast to him. For the Lord is your life, and he will give you many years in the land he swore to give to your fathers, Abraham, Isaac and Jacob.

Gospel
....

Matthew 5:21–37

Here is another reading of contrasts. The "you have heard" passages are contrasted with Jesus' "but I tell you" responses. So as with the previous passage, two readers are needed.

You might also incorporate some movement into this reading, with two people standing behind or beside the readers and "acting" certain parts of the passage (see below) in a simple and graceful manner.

Reader 1: Reads verse 21.

Reader 2: Reads verse 22a, ending with "subject to judgment".

Reader 1: Reads 22b from "again" to "Sanhedrin".

Reader 2: Reads 22c from "but" to "hell", and then verses 23–26.
(In verses 23–24 one person steps forward with a gift in outstretched hands, then turn, embrace the other person and then bring the gift forward. In verses 25–26, one could take the other by the hand, as if leading to court. Then the second could spin the other around, as if taking to the judge. And then a final spin and one falls to the floor as if thrown in jail.)

Reader 1: Reads verse 27.

Reader 2: Reads verses 28–30.
(In verses 29–30, one could pretend to remove an eye and throw away, the other could cut off a hand and throw away.)

Reader 1: Reads verse 31.

Reader 2: Reads verse 32.

Reader 1: Reads verse 33.
(And in verses 33–37, one points to the sky for heaven, to the ground for earth, hands above head in a tower shape for the temple, and both point to each other's head for hair.)

Reader 2: Reads verses 34–37.

PROPER 3
– THE THIRD SUNDAY BEFORE LENT

(In some years, the readings for Proper 3 will be used on the Sunday after Trinity Sunday.)

Psalm
. . . .

Psalm 119:33–40

This reading breaks down nicely into a call-and-response between one reader and the congregation, or between two readers. Because nearly every verse contains "if you do this, Lord… then I will do that", it makes sense to break it up this way, and I hope it will give the congregation a better sense of what this part of the psalm is about.

Reader 1: Reads verse 33a.

Reader 2/Congregation: Reads verse 33b.

Reader 1: Reads first phrase of verse 34 –"Give me understanding".

Reader 2/Congregation: Reads rest of verse 34.

Reader 1: Reads verse 35a.

Reader 2/Congregation: Reads verse 35b.

Reader 1: Reads verse 36a.

Reader 2/Congregation: Reads verse 36b.

Reader 1: Reads verse 37a.

Reader 2/Congregation: Reads verse 37b.

Reader 1: Reads verse 38a.

Reader 2/Congregation: Reads verse 38b.

Reader 1: Reads verse 39a.

Reader 2/Congregation: Reads verse 39b.

Reader 1: Reads verse 40.

Reader 2/Congregation: Reads verse 40b.

Gospel

Matthew 5:38–48

Again, I think that two readers work best here – to demonstrate the contrast between "You have heard" and "I tell you". As with the previous reading two people doing actions at the side or in the background would really work well for this reading.

Reader 1: Reads verse 38.

Reader 2: Reads verses 39–42.

Actions

Verse 39: *One strikes the other who turns and points to face as if to say, "strike me again".*

Verse 40: *One pretends to take garment from the other. The other gives him a second garment.*

Verse 41: *One takes the other by the hand and walks awhile then stops. Then the other takes the hand of the first and walks even further.*

Verse 42: *One asks/begs, the other gives.*

Reader 1: Reads verse 43.

Reader 2: Reads verses 43–48.

Actions

Verse 44: *They fight, or square off to fight, then one grabs and hugs the other.*

Verse 45: *They both look up to heaven as if basking in the sun, then both try to shield themselves from rain or put up umbrellas.*

Verse 46: *They hug, then nod and shrug (when the tax collector is mentioned).*

Verse 47: *They shake hands, then nod and shrug (when the pagans are mentioned).*

Verse 48: *They point to heaven.*

THE SECOND SUNDAY BEFORE LENT

First Reading

Genesis 1:1–2:3

It's easy for the reader to get the congregation to join in with this. You simply tell everyone to repeat what God says after you. So, for example, when you get to "God cried, 'Light!'" you shout it out, and then point to them and get them to shout out "Light!" And it just follows from there. You make a gurgling sound and they do the same, and so on right through the story. This is most effective, I think, if you have a smallish group.

However, if you have a large congregation, it might be fun to break them up into three groups and then move the participation around – pointing to one group and then another to follow you. This works particularly well when you get to the "animal chorus" near the end.

At first, everything was quiet.
   Not a whisper. Not a peep. Not a sound.
   So God cried, "Light!"
   And everything went bright.
   God gurgled, "Sea."
   Gently sighed, "A Pale Blue Sky."
   Then chuckled, "Heavens!" in wonder – and there they were.
   God bellowed next, "Earth!" – deep and loud and strong.
   And out of the deep the mountains rose and the dry land followed along.
   Then God giggled. And the little plants wriggled up out of the ground and began to grow.
   "Bloom!" God boomed. And from their branches sprang flowers and fruit.
   He shouted, "Shining Sun!"
   He howled, "Harvest Moo-oo-oon."
   And when he sang, "Stars," they tinkled and twinkled in tune. *(Everyone says "Twinkle-twinkle" and does the twinkly stars action with hands.)*
   Then God cawed and quacked and shrieked, and a skyful of birds appeared in answer, echoing back his call.

God glugged and chattered and splashed, and a seaful of fish burst through the waves, flipping and flapping in return.

And when he roared and baaed and mooed and mewed, the animals sprang forth and joined his roaring chorus.

"Just one more thing to do," God thought.

And he looked at the dust and whispered, "Hello, Adam."

And he looked again and whispered, "Hello, Eve," as friendly as you like. And when they stood up to greet him, God said:

"This is for you. It's my present. It's noisy, but it's good. Take care of it for me."

And then, his work done, God rested and smiled and said, "Aaaaah!" *(Everyone puts hands behind head as if sleeping and says, "Aaaaah!")*

Gospel

Matthew 6:25–34

For this you will need two readers. The first to read the passage – the words of Jesus – and the second to ask some questions along the way.

Reader 1: "Therefore I tell you, do not worry about your life, what you will eat or drink;"

Reader 2: "But I like to eat and drink. I NEED to eat and drink."

Reader 1: "Or about your body, what you will wear."

Reader 2: "But I need to wear SOMETHING. And as for worrying about my body – everybody worries about their body!"

Reader 1: "Is not life more [important] than food?"

Reader 2: "You said something like that to the devil, once, didn't you?"

Reader 1: "And the body more [important] than clothes?"

Reader 2: "I think you're going to have to unpack this for me."

Reader 1: "Look at the birds of the air;"

Reader 2 *(looking up and pointing)*: "Starlings, sparrows, pigeons *(then wipes face), rotten pigeons!"*

Reader 1: "They do not sow or reap or store away in barns, and yet your heavenly Father feeds them."

Reader 2: "Fair enough – at least as far as the sparrows and starlings go. There's a bird-loving eccentric down the park who feeds the pigeons. But, yes, I get your point."

Reader 1: "Are you not much more valuable than they?"

Reader 2: "I think so, but I have this animal activist friend who might disagree."

Reader 1: "Can any of you by worrying add a single hour to your life?"

Reader 2: "Not me. Not any of us."

Reader 1: "And why do you worry about clothes?"

Reader 2: "Because I like clothes. I've got my eye on this nice pair of trousers. And my wife – you should see the shoes!"

Reader 1: "See how the lilies of the field grow. They do not labour or spin."

Reader 2: "Fair enough. I've never seen a lily do a day's work."

Reader 1: "Yet I tell you that not even Solomon in all his splendour was dressed like one of these."

Reader 2: "I'll have to take your word for that – but, yes, lilies are beautiful, amazing!"

Reader 1: "If that is how God clothes the grass of the field, which is here today and tomorrow is thrown into the fire, will he not much more clothe you – you of little faith?"

Reader 2: "No need to get personal, but, yes, I see your point. It's all about trust, isn't it?"

Reader 1: "So do not worry, saying, 'What shall we eat?' or 'What shall we drink?' or 'What shall we wear?' For the pagans run after all these things, and your heavenly Father knows that you need them."

Reader 2: "So it's all about trust AND priorities. So what should I be concerned about, seek after, and pursue?"

Reader 1: "But seek first his kingdom and his righteousness, and all these things will be given to you as well."

Reader 2: "I see. I've got it. Can't say it's always easy, but I take your point."

Reader 1: "Therefore do not worry about tomorrow, for tomorrow will worry about itself. Each day has enough trouble of its own."

Reader 2: "And on that we can all agree *(then looks up and wipes face)* and there's that blasted pigeon again!"

THE SUNDAY NEXT BEFORE LENT

First reading

Exodus 24:12–18

This is a very simple treatment, but I think it captures the essence of the passage. You will need a reader to read the descriptive lines. And then you will need to divide the congregation into two groups. One group will say the "God came down" lines while simply lowering raised hands. The other group will say the "Moses went up" lines while raising their hands up into the air. Teach the actions and lines before you begin, and if possible put the words on a screen for everyone to follow.

In the thunder and the lightning
God came down

In the shaking and the quaking
God came down

Through the fire and the cloud
God came down

To the top of the mountain
God came down

To give Moses his law
God came down

God came down, and Moses went up
God came down, and Moses went up

In the thunder and the lightning
Moses went up

In the shaking and the quaking
Moses went up

Through the fire and the cloud
Moses went up

To the top of the mountain
Moses went up

To receive God's law
Moses went up

God came down, and Moses went up
God came down, and Moses went up
God came down, and Moses went up

Psalm

....

Psalm 2

You will need three readers for this one. Reader 1 is the voice of the psalmist. Reader 2 is the voice of the nations. Reader 3 is the voice of God.

Reader 1: Reads verses 1–2.

Reader 2: Reads verse 3.

Reader 1: Reads verses 4–5 *(and if Reader 3 can do it without it seeming ridiculous, he can laugh at the appropriate place).*

Reader 3: Reads verse 6.

Reader 1: Reads verse 7, ending at "he said to me".

Reader 3: Reads the rest of verse 7 to the end of verse 9.

Reader 1: Reads verses 10–12.

LENT

ASH WEDNESDAY

Second Reading

2 Corinthians 5:20b – 6:10

I think that using two readers helps to break this passage into more "digestible" bites and also helps the contrasts at the end of the reading to stand out. Like the rest of Paul's letters, it needs to be presented as if you were reading a letter to someone – in a personal, conversational tone. The readers may also want to use subtle actions or movements to communicate the meaning of their lines. But don't make them too "big" and definitely don't make them funny. Consider the day.

Reader 1: We entreat you on behalf of Christ,

Reader 2: Be reconciled to God.

Reader 1: For our sake he made him to be sin

Reader 2: Who knew no sin,

Reader 1: So that in him

Reader 2: We might become the righteousness of God.

Reader 1: As we work together with him, we urge you also not to accept the grace of God in vain. For he says, "At an acceptable time I have listened to you,

Reader 2: And on a day of salvation I have helped you."

Reader 1: See, now is the acceptable time;

Reader 2: See, now is the day of salvation!

Reader 1: We are putting no obstacle in anyone's way, so that no fault may be found with our ministry,

Reader 2: But as servants of God we have commended ourselves in every way:

Reader 1: Through great endurance,

Reader 2: In afflictions,

Reader 1: Hardships,

Reader 2: Calamities,

Reader 1: Beatings,

Reader 2: Imprisonments,

Reader 1: Riots,

Reader 2: Labours,

Reader 1: Sleepless nights,

Reader 2: Hunger,

Reader 1: By purity,

Reader 2: Knowledge,

Reader 1: Patience,

Reader 2: Kindness,

Reader 1: Holiness of spirit,

Reader 2: Genuine love,

Reader 1: Truthful speech,

Reader 2: And the power of God;

Reader 1: With the weapons of righteousness for the right hand

Reader 2: And for the left;

Reader 1: In honour

Reader 2: And dishonour,

Reader 1: In ill repute

Reader 2: And good repute.

Reader 1: We are treated as impostors,

Reader 2: And yet are true;

Reader 1: As unknown,

Reader 2: And yet are well known;

Reader 1: As dying,

Reader 2: And see – we are alive;

Reader 1: As punished,

Reader 2: And yet not killed;

Reader 1: As sorrowful,

Reader 2: Yet always rejoicing;

Reader 1: As poor,

Reader 2: Yet making many rich;

Both readers together *(looking at one another)***:** As having nothing, and yet possessing everything.

Gospel

John 8:1–11

This needs a narrator who will teach the actions and sound-effects beforehand. She then leads the congregation in doing those actions at the appropriate time.

The story begins with a crowd *(do the hubbub/rhubarb crowd noise thing)*. A crowd gathered round Jesus, in the temple courts, waiting for him to speak.

And then there is a surprise *(make surprised gasp – aaah)*. The teachers of the law and the Pharisees bring a woman caught in adultery before Jesus and the crowd.

And then there is a question *(scratch head – look puzzled)*.
"Teacher," they say to Jesus. "The woman standing here before you has been caught committing adultery. The Law of Moses says that such a woman should be stoned to death. What do you say?"

And then there is a bit of a revelation *(say "aha!")*.
(For John, the writer, wants us to know that the question is not genuine. The religious leaders only ask it in the hope of tripping up Jesus.)

Rather surprisingly, this is followed by a bit of composition *(pretend to write)*.
Jesus bends down and, with his finger, writes something in the dirt.

And then a bit of nagging *(prod air with finger)*.
As the Pharisees keep pressing the question.

And then finally, there is an answer *(shout "ta–da!")*.
"If there's anyone here who has never sinned," says Jesus. "Let him throw the first stone."
And then he returns to his essay in the dirt.

At this point there is an exodus *(wave goodbye)*.
(Hey – they're the ones who brought up Moses!) The religious leaders depart, oldest first – and not even one little pebble gets chucked.
And only Jesus and the woman remain.

So then there is another question *(repeat scratching head thing)*.
"Where are they?" Jesus asks the woman. "Is there anyone left to condemn you?"
And she answers simply, "No one."

And so there is a gift *(pretend to give a present)* and a challenge *(swing arm in challenging fashion)*.
"Then I don't condemn you either," says Jesus. "So go – and put your life of sin behind you."

THE FIRST SUNDAY OF LENT

First Reading

Genesis 2:15–17; 3:1–7

Because this passage is essentially a conversation, I think it would be helpful to break it up that way. This both emphasizes the nature of the conversation and also overcomes that "been there, done that" feeling that often accompanies familiar Scripture passages.

So you will need three readers: one for God, one for the woman, and one for the serpent. And I think that it would work with the congregation reading the two narrative verses at the end.

So it breaks down in the following way:

God: Reads Genesis 2, verses 15–17.

Serpent: Reads Genesis 3, verse 1.

Woman: Reads Genesis 3, verses 2–3.

Serpent: Reads Genesis 3, verses 4–5.

Congregation: Reads Genesis 3, verses 6–7.

Gospel

Matthew 4:1–11

A spider skittered under a desert rock.
    A scorpion skipped behind a desert stone.
    A snake slithered across a dusty desert path.
    And then a man sat down, sweating, in the desert heat.
    The man's name was Jesus. He had been wandering through this desert for forty days and forty nights. And he had eaten nothing, for the Spirit of God had called him there to fast.
    The spider dug further beneath the rock.
    The scorpion stopped and raised his tail.
    And the snake stopped, too, and lifted his head from the dust – as if he recognized someone.

For someone was there. There, suddenly, with Jesus. And his name was Satan.

"So they say you're the Son of God," he hissed, his eyes snakelike slits. "If that's the case, you should have no trouble satisfying your aching stomach. Just turn these stones into bread."

Then he picked up a stone and offered it to Jesus. And the spider skittered away in search of another hiding place.

"There are more important things than bread," said Jesus. "Haven't you read what the Scriptures say – 'Man does not live by bread alone, but by every word that comes from the mouth of God.'"

"Ah yes, the Scriptures," Satan smiled. "As it happens, I know them well."

And in a flash, somehow, Satan took them both to the highest point of the temple in Jerusalem.

"The Scriptures say that God will not let you come to harm. That he will send his angels to lift you up, so that your foot will not strike against a stone. So why not jump? And let's see if the Scriptures you cherish so much are true."

Jesus looked down. A long, long way down. A flock of birds flapped by, whistling as they went.

"I think not." Jesus grinned. "For the Scriptures also say that we should trust God and not put him to the test."

And then they were in another place – at the top of a high mountain – and, somehow they were able to see every kingdom of the world.

"I'll give you all of this." Satan laughed. "And all you have to do is bow down and worship me."

But Jesus already had an answer.

"Go away, Satan!" he commanded. "For the Scriptures say that we should worship the Lord our God and serve him only."

So Satan went, and Jesus was back in the desert again.

The spider had buried himself beneath another rock.

The scorpion had lowered his poisonous tail.

Only the snake remained. And as the angels arrived to care for Jesus, it lowered its head back into the dust and slithered sadly away.

THE SECOND SUNDAY OF LENT

Psalm
....

Psalm 121

For this passage, you need either two readers or one reader and the congregation. The first reader asks the question or makes the statement at the beginning of each section (setting the theme for that section), and the second reader responds.

Reader 1: Reads verse 1.

Reader 2/Congregation: Reads verse 2.

Reader 1: Reads verse 3a.

Reader 2/Congregation: Reads verses 3b–4.

Reader 1: Reads verse 5a.

Reader 2/Congregation: Reads verses 5b–6.

Reader 1: Reads verse 7a.

Reader 2: Reads verses 7b–8.

Gospel
....

John 3:1–17

The story begins with a night visit *(SHHHH!)*

A Pharisee called Nicodemus, who also belongs to the Jewish ruling council, comes in the night to meet with Jesus.

It continues with a compliment *(turn to neighbour and say, "You're looking well!")*

"Rabbi," says Nicodemus to Jesus. "We know you're a teacher sent by God because no one could do the miraculous signs you do unless God was with him."

And then there is a puzzle *(scratch head "Huh?").*

Nicodemus seems impressed by the signs he has seen, so Jesus answers him by saying, "I'm telling you the truth – nobody sees the kingdom of God unless he is born again."

And Nicodemus seems completely confused.

"How can you be born when you're old?" he asks. "Can you crawl back into your mother's womb?"

So Jesus gives an explanation *(shout "Aha!")*.

"Nobody enters the kingdom of God unless he's born of water and the Spirit. Flesh comes from flesh, spirit from spirit. You seem surprised when I say that you must be born again. You shouldn't be.

"The wind blows here, the wind blows there, the wind blows wherever it wants. You hear it – but you can't tell where it came from or where it's going. And it's just the same with those who are born of the Spirit."

But Nicodemus is still confused *(scratch head and "Huh?" again)*.

"How can this be?" he asks.

And Jesus gives another explanation *(shout "Aha!" again)*.

"You're one of our nation's leading teachers," he says. "But still you don't get it! I'm only saying what I know to be true – testifying to what I've seen – but you and the other religious leaders still don't accept it. And if you don't believe what I say about things of the earth, how will you believe me when I talk about things of heaven?

"Nobody has ever gone to heaven – except for the one who came from heaven – and that's the Son of Man.

"And just like Moses lifted up the snake in the wilderness, so the Son of Man has to be lifted up. And then everyone who believes in him will have eternal life."

And then Jesus says something that became quite memorable, quite important. So important, in fact, that we are going to have a drum roll and say it together *(do drum roll – hands on laps)*.

Everyone recites John 3:16–17.

THE THIRD SUNDAY OF LENT

First reading

Exodus 17:1–7

You will need three readers and the congregation for this passage. One reader is the narrator, one speaks the words of Moses, one speaks the words of God, and the congregation speaks the words of the people. You might like to tell the congregation that they should read their lines with feeling – as if they really mean them!

Narrator: Reads verses 1–2 ending at "… and said,"

Congregation: Reads verse 2 "Give us water to drink."

Moses: Reads the rest of verse 2.

Narrator: Reads verse 3a ending at "They said,"

Congregation: Reads the rest of verse 3.

Moses: Reads verse 4.

God: Reads verses 5–6 ending at "… for the people to drink."

Narrator: Reads the rest of verses 6 and verse 7 ending at "… tested the Lord saying,"

Congregation: Reads to the end of verse 7.

Second reading

Romans 5:1–11

You will need two readers – one to read the text, and another to lead the congregation in their responses (the bits in the parentheses). My hope is that these responses will, in some sense, punctuate the main emphases of this passage and give a voice to the congregation to celebrate its reality in their lives.

Therefore, since we have been justified through faith,
(through faith!)
we have peace with God
(Peace!)
through our Lord Jesus Christ, through whom we have gained access by
faith into this grace in which we now stand,
(this grace).
And we boast in the hope
(the hope)
of the glory of God. Not only so, but we also glory in our sufferings,
(our sufferings)
because we know that suffering produces perseverance;
(perseverance)
perseverance, character;
(character)
and character, hope.
(hope)
And hope does not put us to shame, because God's love
(God's love)
has been poured out into our hearts through the Holy Spirit,
(the Spirit)
who has been given to us.
You see, at just the right time
(at the right time),
when we were still powerless
(powerless),
Christ died for the ungodly.
(for us)
Very rarely will anyone die for a righteous person, though for a good person
someone might possibly dare to die. But God demonstrates his own love for
us in this: While we were still sinners,
(still sinners)
Christ died for us.
(for us)
Since we have now been justified by his blood, how much more
(how much more)
shall we be saved from God's wrath through him! For if, while we were

God's enemies, we were reconciled to him through the death of his Son,
(his death)
how much more,
(how much more)
having been reconciled, shall we be saved through his life!
(his life)
Not only is this so, but we also boast in God through our Lord Jesus Christ,
through whom we have now received reconciliation.
(through our Lord Jesus Christ!)

THE FOURTH SUNDAY OF LENT

First reading

....

1 Samuel 16:1–13

The story starts with a sad sigh *(sigh sadly)*.

"Samuel," God says, "stop mourning for Saul. I don't want him to be king any more. And that's that.

"So fill up your horn with oil, go to Bethlehem, and visit a man named Jesse. I have chosen one of his sons to take Saul's place."

The story continues with frightened cry *(give a little AAAH!)*.

"But how can I go?" Samuel replies. "Saul will find out I'm there and kill me".

So God comes up with a clever plan *(ta–da!)*.

"Take a cow with you," God says. "Tell everyone you're there to make a sacrifice. Invite Jesse along – and then I will show you which of his sons I want to be the new king. And that's the one you will anoint with oil."

So Samuel takes his cow and his horn full of oil and goes to Bethlehem.

(Sing "O Little Town of Bethlehem…" – not the whole thing, just that line.)

The people are a little nervous when he gets there. They ask him if he has come in peace. But he just follows the plan. "I'm here to make a sacrifice," he says. "Why don't you all join me? Especially you, there, Jesse – and your sons."

So Jesse and his sons come to the sacrifice – all seven of them. *(Hold up seven fingers and say "Perfect!", or if you are in a Darling Buds of May mood –"Perfick!")*

And when Samuel takes a look at Eliab, Jesse's oldest son, he assumes he's found the new king! He's tall, he has muscles, he has muscles on his muscles, and a face that would melt the heart of any woman.

Unfortunately, what he hears from God is the equivalent of one of those "wrong" buzzers *(make wrong buzzer sound)*.

"Ignore his good looks," God says. "And his height. Neither of those did Saul any good, did they? I'm not like you. A person's appearance does not concern me in the least. For I look at what's in their heart."

So Samuel works his way through the other sons *(count to six)*.

And that same buzzer buzzes each time *(buzz six times)*.

So, frustrated, Samuel asks Jesse if he has any other sons.

And suddenly the conversation turns to sheep *(make baaa-ing sound)*.

"Well, there is my youngest, David," says Jesse, "but he's off in the fields, tending the sheep."

"Then send for him!" says Samuel. "We're not going anywhere till he gets here."

So David is sent for. David arrives. He is ruddy and handsome and has a heart keen to do God's will.

And that's when the "right" bell goes off in Samuel's head *(make "ding" sound)*.

"This is the one!" says God. So Samuel anoints him with the oil in front of his brothers. And from that moment God's Spirit comes on him in power – David, God's chosen king.

Gospel

John 9:1–41

You need three people for this. The man born blind (who is also the narrator) and two others to multitask as parents/Jesus/disciples/religious leaders/neighbours.

It will probably be helpful to have simple one-piece props to distinguish the characters. Nothing too complicated – beard for the dad, headscarf mum – or headscarves and so on. I suggest you teach the lines/actions to the congregation first. Or the man born blind could do the "chorus" slowly the first time so people pick things up.

Actions:

"p-tooey"– pretend to spit

"ooey–gooey" – rub fingers together with disgusted look on face

"health and safety" – hold finger in air as if drawing attention to an offence

"halalooey" – wave hands in air in a Pentecostal fashion

Man born blind: I was sitting there on the Sabbath day, born blind and begging, when Jesus and his disciples walked by.

Reader 1 (Disciples): Why is this man blind, teacher? Is it punishment for some bad thing he did or punishment for something his parents did?

Reader 2 (Jesus): Neither. The man wasn't born blind because somebody sinned. This happened so that God could show how powerful he is. You can work when it's light. You can't in the night. But as long as I'm in the world, I'm the light – and I'm here do the work of the one who sent me.

Man born blind: Then Jesus spat on the floor *(p-tooey)*
He made a little mud *(ooey gooey)*
He rubbed it on my eyes *(health and safety!)*
And now I can see *(halalooey!)*
'Cause he's the light of the world.

So I went home, and that's when the neighbours came round

Reader 1 (Neighbour): Tell me, Agnes, isn't this the man born blind?

Reader 2 (Neighbour): That's the one, Huldah – I swear it is.

Reader 1 (Neighbour): No, it only looks like him, Agnes. He's got the same bone structure, but the eyes are set a little too close.

Reader 2 (Neighbour): Right you are, Huldah, and I think his parting was on the other side.

Man born blind: It's me, I said. It's really me. Open your eyes!

Readers 1 & 2 together: Then how come you can see?

Man born blind: So I explained:

Then Jesus spat on the floor *(p-tooey)*
He made a little mud *(ooey gooey)*
He rubbed it on my eyes *(health and safety!)*
And now I can see *(halalooey!)*
'Cause he's the light of the world.

Readers 1 & 2 together: So where is this man who healed you, then?

Man born blind: I don't know, I said. But I could tell they didn't believe me. So they took me to the religious leaders to sort it all out.

Reader 1 (Pharisee): So this healing you say you experienced – it happened on the Sabbath, did it?

Reader 2 (Pharisee): But on the Sabbath, no one is allowed to work.

Reader 1 (Pharisee): So the man who made you see broke the Sabbath rules?

Reader 2 (Pharisee): And therefore cannot be a good man at all!

Reader 1 (Pharisee): On the other hand, if he is a sinner…

Reader 2 (Pharisee): … how did he perform this miracle?

Man born blind: They were puzzled, obviously – so they asked me what I thought. And I said:

Then Jesus spat on the floor *(p-tooey)*
He made a little mud *(ooey gooey)*
He rubbed it on my eyes *(health and safety!)*
And now I can see *(halalooey!)*
'Cause he's the light of the world.

But that didn't go down well, either.

Reader 1 (Pharisee): I bet this man was never blind at all.

Reader 2 (Pharisee): And this is some kind of clever trick.

Readers 1 & 2 together: Fetch his parents!

Man born blind: And so they did.

Reader 1 (Dad): Blind from birth he was. Blind as a doorpost.

Reader 2 (Mum): That's deaf, dear. It's "blind as a bat".

Reader 1 (Dad): I hate bats. They give me the creeps. I just want to smack them.

Reader 2 (Mum): With a bat, dear?

Reader 1 (Dad): With a doorpost. Heh-heh. They'd never hear me coming.

Man born blind: In the end, they were no help at all.

Reader 2: Completely batty!

Man born blind: They told the religious leaders that I was old enough to speak for myself. So I did. Or at least I tried…

For the *(counts one-two-three)* fourth time:

Then Jesus spat on the floor *(p-tooey)*
He made a little mud *(ooey gooey)*
He rubbed it on my eyes *(health and safety!)*
And now I can see *(halalooey!)*
'Cause he's the light of the world.

Why do you keep asking? I said. Do you want to become his disciples, too?

Reader 1 (Pharisee): Don't be ridiculous.

Reader 2 (Pharisee): We don't know anything about this Jesus!

Man born blind: Really? You know nothing about him? I was blind, I can see. Open your eyes – only someone from God could do something like that!

Reader 1 (Pharisee): And what do you know?

Reader 2 (Pharisee): Throw him out!

Man born blind: So there I was, back where I started. Back on the street. And that's when Jesus came by again.

Reader 2 (Jesus): Do you believe in the Son of Man?

Man born blind: Who's that? Tell me, so I can believe in him.

Reader 2 (Jesus): You're looking at him. He's the one speaking to you.

Man born blind: Then I do believe. I really do. Thank you for helping me see.

Reader 2 (Jesus): That's why I came into the world – so the blind can see – and so those who think they can see will discover that they are really blind.

Reader 1 (Dad): Blind as doorposts!

Reader 2 (Mum): Couldn't have put it better myself.

Man born blind: Well that's not me, because *(all do it together):*

Then Jesus spat on the floor *(p-tooey)*
He made a little mud *(ooey gooey)*
He rubbed it on my eyes *(health and safety!)*
And now I can see *(halalooey!)*
'Cause he's the light of the world.

MOTHERING SUNDAY

First reading

....

Exodus 2:1–10

The congregation can have some fun joining in with sound effects and actions when they hear these words or phrases:

"Wet" – say "Ooh" and make a drippy, shaking water from your hands action.
"Boring" – yawn widely.
"Looking bad" – say "Uh-oh".
"Looking even worse" – make a bigger "Uh-oh" sound.
"Looking better" – say "Whew!"
"Time to do something" – look at watch.
"Time to wonder" – say "Wow!"

What was it like at the edge of the river?
　　It was wet.
　　Squishy toe wet.
　　Soggy bottom wet.
　　Hot-and-muggy sweaty wet.
　　The girl peered through the reeds. They sprouted thick and tall from the riverbank mud.
　　The girl peered out onto the river at a bobbing bulrush boat. She hoped that, at least, her brother was dry.
　　What was it like at the edge of the river?
　　It was wet.

What was it like at the edge of the river?
　　It was boring.
　　She was supposed to watch her brother. That's what her mother had said. She was supposed to make sure that nothing happened to him. She was supposed to just sit there and wait.
　　But for how long?
　　Till Pharaoh, king of Egypt, decided to stop killing all the baby Hebrew boys? Till her little brother started to outgrow his bulrush boat? Till his arms

poked through the sides, and his legs poked through the end, and his head popped out the top?

The girl laughed when she thought of that. It was nice to laugh for a change.

Better than being bored.

Better than sitting leg–stiff still.

Better than staring, eyes tired and sore.

Better than nodding off, eyelids drooping and chin dropping onto her chest.

What was it like at the edge of the river?

It was boring.

What was it like at the edge of the river?

It was looking bad.

The girl's long wait was broken by the sound of voices.

The riverbank reeds were broken by tramping feet.

And the hot sweat of boredom broke into a cold sweaty fear.

The girl crouched down as low as she could, so she could see without being seen.

What she saw were women.

What she saw were Egyptian women.

What she saw were Egyptian women walking alongside the river, right towards her baby brother in his bulrush boat!

If they find him, she thought, they'll kill him.

But what could she do?

She was too small to fight them. She was too slow to reach him and pull him back to shore. And there was no time to run for help.

What was it like at the edge of the river?

It was looking bad.

What was it like at the edge of the river?

It was looking even worse!

The baby started to cry. The women started to point. And then one of them waded out into the river, pulled the bulrush boat out of the water and carried it back to shore.

The other women gathered round and blocked the girl's view. Now she was more helpless than ever!

And then the girl remembered. She remembered the stories her mother had told her about God.

The God who had led Abraham to a special land.

The God who had protected Joseph from the anger of his brother.

The God who had saved Joseph from another pharaoh's prison.

Maybe, just maybe, she thought, God could save her baby brother, too.

"Please, God," she prayed, "don't let them hurt him."

At last, the women moved away and the girl could see her little brother again.

He wasn't dead.

He wasn't hurt.

He wasn't even crying.

In fact, one of the women was holding him and hugging him and stroking his head.

What was it like at the edge of the river?

It was looking better!

What was it like at the edge of the river?

It was time to do something.

If those Egyptian women were not going to hurt her brother, then the girl wanted to know what they did intend to do with him. So she crept towards them, her head below the reeds and her ears wide open.

"I am Pharaoh's daughter," she heard one of the women say. "I can do what I please. And what pleases me is to adopt this Hebrew child as my own. What I need is some woman to feed him and care for him until he is old enough to come and live with me."

Like a pheasant spooked by a dog, like a puppet on a stage, like a Jack-in-the-box (or better still, a Jill-in-the-box!), the girl popped up out of the reeds.

"I know a woman," she said, "who would be just perfect for that job. She doesn't live far from here, and I am sure that she would love and care for your baby as if he were her very own!"

What was it like at the edge of the river?

It was time to do something.

What was it like at the edge of the river?

It was time to wonder.

"All right," said the Egyptian to the girl. "Go and fetch this woman.

Say that Pharaoh's daughter commands her to care for..." And, here, she paused. "For little 'Pulled Out'. For I pulled him out of the water!"

The girl nodded, then turned and ran quickly home.

How wonderful! Her brother was safe!

More wonderful still – his own mother would be able to care for him!

But what a silly name. Little "Pulled Out".

What was the Egyptian word for that? "Moses."

And then, the girl thought, maybe it wasn't so silly. Maybe her brother's new name was a wonder, too. For hadn't she prayed? And hadn't the God of her fathers heard her prayer and pulled little Moses out of trouble? Like he'd pulled Abraham and Jacob and Joseph out of trouble, all those years ago.

God had pulled them out to do something special with them. And so the girl wondered. Had God pulled out Moses to do something special with him, as well?

What was it like at the edge of the river?

It was time to wonder.

First reading (alternative)

1 Samuel 1:20–28

Hannah was barren. And in the time and the place that Hannah lived, to be barren was to be cursed.

But things are not always what they look like.

Situations are not always what they seem.

And God has a way of taking one thing and turning it into something completely different.

Hannah was married to Elkanah – a man of means who could afford a second wife – Peninnah. And Peninnah, as it happens, was not barren at all. She had a brood of children, which she stood before Hannah, at every opportunity, to make her curse even worse.

Elkanah was a good man. He saw, he understood, he longed to ease Hannah's pain. So when the family trooped from their home in Ramah to the holy place at Shiloh each year, and when they sat down to eat a portion of the meat that had been offered as a sacrifice to God, Elkanah always made sure that Hannah got a double helping of that meat – a special treat and, surely, the first recorded example of comfort eating.

In spite of all her children, however (and as a powerful argument for monogamy!), Peninnah was jealous of this simple act of kindness. And she did all she could to make that a curse, as well.

"It is God who has closed your womb," she would tell Hannah, there, in the presence of God himself, in his own holy place. And she would do this, not once, not twice, but again and again and again, right up to the time of the feast. And poor Hannah would be so upset that she could not enjoy the treat her husband had planned for her. In fact, she could not eat at all.

"Eat, Hannah, eat!" Elkanah would say. He meant well, but (being a man!) he ended up saying all the things a husband should never say to his wife when she is so unhappy she can't eat.

"Why are you crying?

"Why are you so upset?

"You may not have any children – but you have me!"

One year, Hannah was so upset that she left the table altogether. She went to the door of the holy place, where Eli the priest was sitting. And there, through her tears, she offered up a prayer to God.

"Look at me, Lord, please! See my misery. Remember my condition. And give me a son, I pray. For if you do, then I will give him back to you, and dedicate him as your servant for all the days of his life."

These words were hard words. So hard that she could not speak them out loud. Hannah's lips moved, her tears flowed, and the old priest Eli (another man!) assumed that she was drunk.

"Sober up, woman!" he said. "This is neither the time nor the place. Take your bottle and go home!"

Hannah could not believe this. All she wanted was help, and here was another curse.

"Drunk?" she cried. "Is that what you think? I'm not drunk! In fact, I can hardly eat or drink a thing! I'm here to pray – that's all – to pour out my grief and my troubles before the Lord."

"I see," said Eli, sorry not only for her sadness but for his mistake as well. "Then go in peace. And may the God of Israel give you what you asked for."

It was a blessing. A blessing, at last. Hard won, to be sure. But a blessing and not a curse.

So Hannah went.

And Hannah had something to eat.

And when she saw her husband, she smiled.

And when they returned to Ramah, she lay with him and conceived and gave birth to a son and called him Samuel – a name which means "God heard me".

And when Samuel was old enough, she took him back to Shiloh, back to the old priest Eli.

And though it sounds like the act of a crazy woman, or a drunk woman, she left her only son there to serve in the holy place.

A blessing in return for a blessing.

A blessing, not a curse.

THE FIFTH SUNDAY OF LENT

First reading

Ezekiel 37:1–14

This reading is accompanied by some simple actions made by the reader.

My story begins with bones
(say "bones" but in a scary, creepy, ghost story kind of way)

The Spirit of the Lord took me to the middle of a valley – a valley filled with bones.

And there, in the valley, he led me on a walk
(make a slow walking motion)

And I walked through the bones, here and there, across the valley. Thousands and thousands of bones. Dry, dry bones.

Then he asked me a question
(say "A question?")

"Son of man, Do you think that these bones can live?"

And I said, "Lord, you, alone, know the answer to that." So he answered.

"Prophesy!" he told me.
(extend hand as if addressing the crowd – say "Prophesy!")

"Prophesy to the bones," he told me. "Say to the bones, 'hear what God has to say to you.

   'I will attach tendons to you. And muscle and skin to you. I will put my breath in you. You will come to life. And you will know that I am God!'"

So I prophesied to the bones as I was told. And as I spoke, I heard a rattling sound…
(make rattling sound – tap on back of chairs)

And the bones began to come together – bone to bone to bone. And then tendons. And then muscle. And then skin. And now, instead of bones, the valley was covered with bodies. Thousands and thousands of dead bodies.

For there was no breath in them.

So God spoke again. "Prophesy," he said to me, "prophesy to the breath."
(make a whooshing sound)

"Come from the four winds – from north and south and east and west.
Come, breath – and breathe into the dead so they may live!"

So I did as I was told. I prophesied to the breath. And the breath came
(whooosh again)

It entered the dead bodies. They came to life. They stood before me – and
now the valley was covered with a vast, vast army!

And then God spoke to me again about the bones
(say "the bones" in that creepy way again)

"The bones," he said, "are the people of Israel. They say that they are dried
up like the bones, hopeless like the bones, cut off from life like the bones.
So I want you to prophesy to the people of Israel."

*(As you do the following lines and actions, get bigger and bigger and more
excited.)*

"Tell them that I am going to open their graves"
*(reach down and pretend to open door in floor – while saying "open their
graves")*

 "Tell them that I am going to bring them up from their graves"
*(reach down into pretend grave and pull someone out – while saying "bring
them up from their graves")*

"Tell them that I am going to put my Spirit in them and they will live"
(whoosh sound again)

"Tell them that I am going to take them back to their land"
*(pretend to take someone by hand and lead – while saying "take them back
to their land")*

"And then they will know that I am God and that I have spoken.
For I will make their dry bones"
(say "bones" again)

"Live!"
(whooshing sound)

Gospel

....

John 11:1–45

You will need six readers at the front, from left to right – Mary, Martha, Lazarus, Jesus, disciples, onlookers – and a narrator off to one side.

Narrator: Lazarus was ill.

Lazarus: *Achoo!*

Narrator: No, I mean really ill.

Lazarus: Bigger *Achoo!*

Narrator: No, I mean really, really ill.

Lazarus: Huge *Achoo!*

Narrator: He lived in Bethany. With his sister Martha… *(Martha waves.)*

Narrator: And his sister Mary, who poured perfume on Jesus and wiped his feet with her hair. *(Mary points to her hair.)*

Narrator: Mary and Martha sent word to Jesus that their brother was ill.

Mary and Martha together: Lord, the one you love is ill.

Lazarus: *Achoo!*

Mary and Martha: No, really ill.

Lazarus: Bigger *Achoo!*

Mary and Martha: No, really, really ill.

Lazarus: Huge *Achoo!*

Narrator: When he got the message, Jesus said…

Jesus: "This illness is not going to end in death. It's for God's glory, so God's Son might be glorified."

Narrator: Jesus loved Mary and Martha and Lazarus. He really did. But he waited for two days before he went to see them. He said to his disciples:

Jesus: "Time for us to go back to Judea."

Narrator: But the disciples were not so keen on that idea.

Disciples: "We were just there – and they tried to stone you. Why would you want to go back?"

Narrator: So Jesus answered them:

Jesus: "There are twelve hours of daylight, right? If you walk in the day, you won't stumble – because you can see by this world's light. It's only at night that you stumble, for there is no light."

Narrator: Then Jesus went on to say:

Jesus: "Lazarus, our friend, has fallen asleep."*(Lazarus snores.)*

Jesus: "And I am going there so I can wake him up."

Disciples: "If Lazarus is asleep…"*(Lazarus snores.)*

Disciples: "That means he will get better."

Lazarus: *(Opens one eye)* "Yipee!"

Narrator: But the disciples were wrong. They thought that Jesus was talking about natural sleep. But he was really trying to say that Lazarus had died.

Lazarus: "What? Rats! UURCK" *(Tilts head and dies – and then stays that way with his head tilted till he comes back to life again.)*

Jesus: "No, I mean that Lazarus is dead. And, in a way, that's a good thing for you, because this is going to help you believe. Let's go."

Narrator: And that's when Thomas, one of the disciples, said:

Disciples: "Yeah, right, let's go to Judea – so we can all die with him."

Narrator: So off they went. And by the time they got to Bethany, Lazarus had been in the tomb for four days. Bethany was only two miles from Jerusalem, so Mary and Martha had already received comfort from quite a few visitors.

When Martha heard that Jesus was coming, she went outside the village to meet him on his way. But Mary stayed in the house.

And that's when Martha and Jesus had a little chat.

Martha: "If you'd been here, Lord, my brother Lazarus would not have died. But I know that God can still give you whatever you ask from him."

Jesus: "Martha, your brother will rise again."

Martha: "I know he will. At the resurrection. On the last day."

Jesus: "Martha, I am the resurrection and the life. The one who believes in me will live, even if he dies. And whoever lives and believes in me will never die. Do you believe that?"

Martha: "I do. You are the Christ, the Son of God, the one that God promised to send into this world."

Narrator: After this, Martha went back to the house to talk to Mary.

Martha (*turning to Mary*)**:** "The teacher's here. He wants to see you."

Narrator: So Mary left the house and went to the same place, outside the village, to see Jesus. And the guests who had come from Jerusalem to comfort her went with her, thinking that she was going to the tomb to mourn.
    When Mary saw Jesus, she fell at his feet and said the same thing as Martha.

Mary: "If you'd been here, Lord, my brother Lazarus would not have died."

Narrator: When Jesus saw her weeping, and the visitors weeping with her, he was deeply moved and troubled.
    And he simply asked

Jesus: "Where is he buried?"

Others: "Come and see."

Narrator: And that's when Jesus wept. And when the visitors saw it, they couldn't help but remark. Some said:

Others: "He must have loved Lazarus very much."

Narrator: While others said:

Others: "He opened the eyes of the blind. He could have kept this man from dying."

Narrator: So they took Jesus to the tomb – a cave, with a stone across the entrance. And still weeping, he said:

Jesus: "Take away the stone."

Martha: "But, Lord, he's been in there four days. The smell…"

Jesus: "Remember what I told you. That you would see the glory of God – if you would only believe."

Narrator: So they took away the stone. And Jesus looked up and said:

Jesus: "Thank you for hearing me, Father. Yes, I know that you always hear me – but the people standing here need to know that, so they will believe that you sent me."

Narrator: Then Jesus shouted:

Jesus: "Lazarus, Come out!"

Narrator: And Lazarus came out.

Lazarus: "What? Really?"

Narrator: Yes, Lazarus came out – with the grave clothes wrapped around him and a cloth around his face. Because Lazarus was alive!

Lazarus (*shouts*): "I'm alive!"

Narrator: Really alive.

Lazarus (*even louder shout*): "I'm alive!"

Narrator: Really, really alive.

Lazarus: "I'm alive." (*hugs sisters, high fives the others*) "I'm alive. I'm alive. I'm alive!"

Jesus: "Remove those grave clothes. Let him go!"

Narrator: And so many of the visitors who came to comfort Mary and Martha saw what Jesus did – and came to believe in him, too.

PALM SUNDAY

First reading

Isaiah 50:4–9a

I love all the references to body parts in this passage. Why not get the congregation to repeat each part and point to it when you get there. For example, in verse 4, after the reader reads "instructed tongue" the congregation points to open mouth and says "tongue". They could be led in this either by the reader or an assistant – and they need it explained before the reading – and maybe even projected up front, so they can follow more easily.

Reader: Reads verse 4.
(Congregation says "tongue" and point to tongue, and "ear" and point to ear, as appropriate.)

Reader: Reads verse 5.
(Congregation says "ears" and point to ears.)

Reader: Reads verse 6.
(Congregation puts hands on back and says "back", points to cheek and says "cheek", puts hand on face and says "face". If anyone has a beard they might like to have some fun with this.)

Reader: Reads verse 7.
(Congregation puts hand on face and says "face".)

Reader: Reads verse 8.
(Congregation might like to repeat the hand on face action. Even though it's used as a verb here, the play on words is kind of fun!)

Second reading

Philippians 2:5–11

This passage is all about movement. Jesus humbles himself; he comes down. Jesus is exalted; he goes up. So the reading will be punctuated by the movement of the congregation coming down and going up.

When I do this reading, I usually begin by explaining what I am going to do and then suggesting that it's not meant to be a test of leg and back strength, and that anyone who feels like sitting right down, should feel free to do so. This is especially true if you have an older congregation – don't want any legs cramping along the way.

It goes without saying that the reader (or a very visible assistant) also needs to move down and up so the congregation knows when to move.

If you want to make it harder (but also that bit more dramatic) move down at the end of verse 6 and then halfway through 7, then at the end, halfway through 8, then at the end – at those places where Jesus "moves down". And then split it up the same way when he is exalted.

Read verses 5–8. *(The reading begins with the congregation standing. They gradually move down towards their seats – getting that bit lower at the end of verse 6, verse 7 and verse 8 – until by the end of verse 8 they are sitting down.)*

Read verses 9–11. *(The congregation reverses the motion– creeping up little by little – until by the end of verse 11 they are standing again.)*

Gospel
....

Matthew 21:1–11

It starts with Jesus and his disciples – approaching Jerusalem from the Mount of Olives. It starts slow and quiet. Quiet as a midnight heist *(have everyone go "SHHH")*.

And even though what happens next is technically not a robbery – it sure sounds like one.

"Go into the village," says Jesus. "You'll find a donkey there, tied up next to its colt. Untie them and bring them to me. And if anyone says anything, tell him that I need them, and everything will be okay."

And you've got to wonder, haven't you? Was this donkey-borrowing a normal sort of thing? Was Jesus just hoping no one would notice? Were his instructions given "just in case"? Or had he prearranged it all?

Somebody had certainly prearranged it, because Matthew says that all this donkey-borrowing/nicking/riding stuff was the fulfilment of something that the prophet Isaiah had said hundreds of years before.

> *"Say to Zion's daughter*
> *Look, here comes your king*
> *He's gentle and he's riding on a donkey*
> *On a colt, a donkey's foal."*

So the disciples do what Jesus asks. They acquire the donkey and the colt without incident (in Matthew's version, anyway). They put their cloaks on them. And Jesus hops aboard.

And now things get a little noisier *(have everyone make a noisy crowd hubbub sound)*. A crowd gathers. A very large crowd. Some of them spread their cloaks on the road in front of him. Others cut branches from trees and spread those in front, as well.

And now things are getting really loud *(have everyone do a big cheer)*.

The crowd shouts:

"Hosanna to the Son of David" *(everyone repeats)*
"Blessed is he who comes in the name of the Lord" *(everyone repeats)*
"Hosanna in the highest" *(everyone repeats)*.

And by the time this procession reaches Jerusalem, the whole city is asking, "Who is this?"

And the crowd answers:

"This is the prophet from Nazareth in Galilee" *(everyone repeats loudly)*
"THIS IS JESUS!" *(everyone repeats with a shout)*.

HOLY WEEK

MONDAY OF HOLY WEEK

Gospel

John 12:1–11

The story begins with a dinner *(rub tummy – MMMM)*.

A dinner in Bethany, six days before the Passover.
A dinner at the home of Mary and Martha.
A dinner in honour of Jesus, because he had raised their brother Lazarus from the dead.

The story continues with the smell of perfume *(inhale deeply, then go "AAAAH" or "Lovely!")*.

Jesus is reclining at the table.
Lazarus is reclining there, too.
Martha is serving the food.
And Mary? Mary brings out a jar of perfume, pure nard, incredibly expensive, pours it on Jesus' feet, then wipes his feet with her hair!
And the fragrance fills the house.

But there is an objection *(raise finger in air – "I object!")*.

Judas Iscariot (who will later betray Jesus) says,
"This perfume was worth a year's wages! Why wasn't it sold – and the money given to the poor?"

Which all sounds very good and holy and Jesus-friendly – except for Judas's dirty little secret *(finger to mouth – SHHHH)*.

(In a whisper) He's the treasurer of the group you see. He watches over the money. But when nobody is watching, he helps himself to the odd fiver or tenner or whatever he can get away with. He doesn't care for the poor at all.

So Jesus responds to his objection *(pretend to bang gavel – "Objection overruled!").*

"Let her be," he says. "This perfume was meant to be used for my burial. And as for the poor – they will always be here. I can't say the same for me."

Meanwhile, there is a commotion outside *(hubbub, crowd sounds).*

Word of the dinner has spread throughout the region. And a large crowd has gathered to see Jesus and the man he raised from the dead.

And so there is another dirty little secret *(finger to mouth and SHHHHH again).*

So many people have put their faith in Jesus because of what he did, that the chief priests make plans to kill him – and Lazarus too.

TUESDAY OF HOLY WEEK

Gospel

John 12:20–36

Strictly speaking, today's reading begins at verse twenty, but Jesus' entry into Jerusalem very much sets the stage for it, which is why it is also part of the reading.

You either need to divide the congregation into six groups, with each group doing one of the lines below, or you will need to teach the whole group the six lines and let them all join in the fun each time. Alternatively, you could also have seven readers – a narrator and six for the other lines, but I think that including the congregation works best.

First, teach these lines and actions:

1 The crowd**:** "Hosanna! Blessed is he who comes in the name of the Lord." *(Wave your pretend palm branches and shout.)*
2 The disciples**:** "Huh? What? We don't get it." *(Scratch your head in thought.)*
3 The people who saw Lazarus raised: "Amazing, incredible, unbelievable – and a little stinky." *(Hold your nose.)*
4 The Pharisees: "It looks like the whole world is following him." *(Shake head and sigh.)*
5 The Greeks: "We want hummus!" *(Throw an imaginary plate on the floor.)*
6 The voice of God: "I am glorified and I will be glorified again." *(Make your voice as big and deep as possible.)*

The reader's text is below, with the shared lines in italic.

The crowd that had come for the Passover festival heard that Jesus was coming into Jerusalem. So they grabbed palm branches and waved them. And they shouted:
 1 "Hosanna. Blessed is he who comes in the name of the Lord."

Jesus was riding on a young donkey. He did this to fulfil the words of the prophet: Do not be afraid, Daughter of Zion, see, your king is coming seated on a donkey's colt. His disciples didn't understand this.

2 *"Huh? What? We don't get it."*

But once Jesus came back from the dead and ascended into heaven, they realized what it was all about. The people who had seen his friend Lazarus raised from the dead kept talking about it.

3 *"Amazing, incredible, unbelievable – and a little stinky!"*

So the people they had talked to came out to meet Jesus, too. And the Pharisees? The Pharisees were distraught.

4 *"It looks like the whole world is following him."*

Which wasn't far from the truth – and very much part of the plan! You see, there were Greeks at the festival too.

5 *"We want hummus!"*

And they asked to see Jesus. And when Jesus chatted with them, this is what he said.

"The time has come for me to be glorified. For a grain of wheat to make more wheat, it has to die. Try to hang onto your life and you will lose it. Give it away and you will keep it forever. And if you want to serve me, then you will have to treat your life in just the same way. And that will honour the Father.

"I'm troubled. I admit it. Do I ask the Father to save me from what lies ahead? No. That's what I came for. And so I will do what I have come for – and God will be glorified by it.

Then a voice came from heaven and said:

6 *"I am glorified and I will be glorified again."*

The crowd thought it was thunder or the voice of an angel. Jesus said, "The voice was for you, not me. It's time for the world to be judged, time for the devil to be defeated. For when I am lifted up, I will draw all people to myself."

Jesus said this to show what kind of death he would die.

But, in response, the crowd spoke up again.

1 *"Hosanna. Blessed is he who comes in the name of the Lord."*

They were just a little confused. A bit like the disciples.

2 *"Huh? What? We don't get it."*

"The law says that the Messiah will live forever. Why do you say that the Son of Man must be lifted up? And who is this Son of Man?"

So Jesus answered them.

"You are only going to have the light with you for a little while longer. So walk while the light is shining – before the darkness comes. If you walk in the dark, you don't know where you're going. So walk in the light while it's shining – and you will become sons of light."

And then he left them and hid himself from them.

WEDNESDAY OF HOLY WEEK

Second reading

....

Hebrews 12:1–3

I know that, strictly speaking, we're the ones who need to be looking at "the cloud of witnesses" as our inspiration and example, rather than the other way round. But I thought it would be nice to push the racing imagery and have it both ways! Cheering is the key participation device here. Everyone could do it together (either at the end of "cheering" or at the end of the first line), or you could divide the congregation into groups and work your way along, to make the cheer louder, in a kind of "wave" cheer.

> *They're cheering. Can you hear them?*
> *Like a cloud, they surround us.*
> *The ones who've run the race before.*
>
> *Abel and Enoch,*
> *Noah and Abraham,*
> *Isaac and Jacob and Joseph and Moses.*
>
> *Look at them training.*
> *Take note of their technique.*
> *They'll teach us how to run the race.*
>
> *They're cheering. Can you hear them?*
> *Like a cloud, they surround us.*
> *The ones who've run the race before.*
>
> *Rahab and Gideon,*
> *Barak and Samson,*
> *Jephthah and David and Samuel and the prophets*
>
> *Throw off everything that holds you back.*
> *Like Noah threw off his doubt,*

Like Abraham threw off his homeland,
Like Enoch threw off the weight of the world and went to walk with God.

Throw off whatever is wrong, as well – whatever tempts and tangles and trips you up.
Like Rahab threw off her idols,
Like Jacob threw off his deceit,
Like Moses threw off the pleasures of sin and chose the plight of his people.

Then run with perseverance. Run the whole course and never give up.
Like Joseph waiting for his dreams to come true,
Like Samuel searching for a king,
Like Gideon watching his army weaken to point he could claim God's victory.

They're cheering. Can you hear them?
Like a cloud, they surround us.
The ones who've run the race before. (Somewhere, in the background, "Chariots of Fire" music is playing.)

And out in front, out in front of us all
Is the one on whom we fix our eyes.
He's setting the pace. He's leading the race.
The author and perfecter of our faith.

He hurdles the shame,
He fights through the pain.
It looks like the race will be lost.
But in spite of his foes
He endures, wins, then throws
His arms wide in the shape of a cross.

So let's run the race.
Run and not grow weary.
Run for the prize that's set before us.

And when we get run down,
Let's look and let's listen.
For we don't run this race alone.

They're cheering. Can you hear them?
Like a cloud, they surround us.
The ones who've run the race before.

MAUNDY THURSDAY

Second Reading

1 Corinthians 11:23–26

I received it. I don't keep it to myself. I pass it on.

Jesus faces betrayal. The betrayal of a friend. But it does not kill friendship for him.

So he sits among his friends. He takes a piece of bread. He says "Thank you." He breaks it.

Then he shares it. Among his friends. And he shares himself. Vulnerable. Broken. Betrayed.

"This is my body. But it's for you. Remember me, when you eat it."

Then, when his friends have finished their supper, he takes a cup. He shares that, too.

"This cup is a new covenant, agreement, relationship – that's it. Relationship. That thing that goes on between friends. And it's sealed by my blood. Remember me when you drink it."

So let's eat the bread, friends.

And let's drink from the cup, friends.

Even though there are none of us that have been completely faithful friends.

And let's proclaim with one voice that Jesus died for us.

Until we join him at another table. Forever friends.

Gospel

John 13:1–7, 31b–35

The reader reads the first line of each couplet three times, then he (or a second reader) reads the *second* line, with the congregation joining in the sounds or actions – also three times. It helps to teach the actions before you start the story. Not only is it a kind of reinforcement, but it also helps everyone feel that bit more secure because they know what's coming.

Jesus and his disciples came together for a meal. *(x3)*
The food was served; it was almost time to eat *("mmm"). (x3)*

But dusty roads make for sweaty toes *(x3)*
And their toes weren't smelling very sweet *("phee-ewe"). (x3)*

So Jesus grabbed a towel and poured water in a basin *(x3)*
Then went to wash his disciples' feet *("scrub-a-dub"). (x3)*

But when he came to Peter, Peter said "You'll not wash me *(x3)*
You're my master, not my servant, take your seat!"*(point, as if pointing at seat). (x3)*

"Unless I wash you," Jesus said, "you'll have no part of me *(x3)*
Don't you see, it's my sacrifice, my treat" *(hold out hands). (x3)*

"Then Lord," said Simon Peter, "wash me, wash me how you will *(x3)*
Wash me, head and hands and feet and all – complete" *(point to individual parts and then run hands down body). (x3)*

"There's a lesson here," said Jesus, when the washing was all done *(x3)*
"To remember, to make note of, or to Tweet"*(mime tweeting with your thumbs). (x3)*

"A servant is not greater than his master," Jesus said *(x3)*
"No better than the man in the driver's seat" *(make driving motion). (x3)*

"So if I, your Lord and Teacher can bend down and scrub your toes *(x3)*
Then you can also wash each others' feet" *("scrub-a-dub"). (x3)*

Reader 1: "Now come on, my friends, I think it's time to eat" *("mmm").*

GOOD FRIDAY

Second Reading

Hebrews 4:14–16; 5:7–9

Reader: Jesus is our high priest. He's the Son of God. He's gone through the heavens.

Congregation: So let's hold on, firmly, to what we believe.

Reader: He understands our weaknesses. He's been tempted, just like us. But he never sinned. He's sympathetic. He understands. His throne is a throne of grace.

Congregation: So let's go to it, confident that we'll find mercy when we need it.

Reader: When Jesus was on earth, he prayed to God with tears and loud cries, prayed to be saved from death.

Congregation: And God heard him because he was willing to do whatever God wanted, in the end.

Reader: He was God's son, yes, but still he was willing to suffer for us.

Congregation: And his willingness to obey sourced salvation forever for those who are willing to obey him!

Psalm

Psalm 22

I think the contrasts in this psalm are best served by using two readers at the front. And because they both speak for the psalmist – for his alternating viewpoint between his predicament and what he knows about God – I would have them stand close together, or back to back. As with many of the passages, it's helpful to explain why the passage will be broken up this way.

Alternatively, you could have one reader and the congregation, in which case, I would suggest letting the reader take those parts that deal with the psalmist's predicament (the Reader 1 below).

Reader 1: Reads verses 1–2.

Reader 2/Congregation: Reads verses 3–5.

Reader 1: Reads verses 6–8.

Reader 2/Congregation: Reads verses 9–11.

Reader 1: Reads verses 12–18.

Reader 2/Congregation: Reads verses 19–31.

EASTER EVE

First reading

Job 14:1–14

Try having the readers in different places. Reader 1 sits and reader 2 stands behind. Or perhaps, reader 1 stands and the reader 2 stands in some higher place – up in the pulpit, possibly, depending on your furniture!

Reader 1: Reads verses 1–6.

Reader 2: Reads verses 7–12 (looking down at Reader 1 as she reads verses 10–12).

Reader 1: Reads verses 13–14.

Gospel

Matthew 27:57–66

Jesus is dead.
Evening is coming.
So a rich man from Arimathea,
Joseph.
One of Jesus' disciples.
Asks Pilate for his body.

Jesus is dead.
Pilate agrees.
And Jesus' body is given to Joseph.

Jesus is dead.
So Joseph takes his body.
He wraps it in a linen cloth.
He places it in his own tomb
A new tomb
Hewn out of a rock.

And he rolls a stone in front of it
While Mary and Mary sit and watch.

Jesus is dead.
But there is this rumour
That three days will pass
And he will rise again.
So just like Joseph,
The Pharisees pay Pilate a visit.

Jesus is dead.
For three days
We need guards around the tomb
In case his disciples steal his body,
Pretend that he has risen,
And complete his deceit.

Jesus is dead.
So Pilate gives the order,
Guards are sent,
The tomb is sealed,
Everything is secure.

Jesus is dead.
They watch and they wait.
Two days gone,
One more day to go…

EASTER

EASTER VIGIL

Canticle

Exodus 15:1b–13, 17–18

You will either need one reader and the congregation, or two readers for this one. I have broken it up so that the first reader essentially expresses the theme of each section and the second reader/congregation "unpacks" that theme.

Reader 1: Reads verse 1b.

Reader 2/Congregation: Reads verse 1c.

Reader 1: Reads verse 2a.

Reader 2/Congregation: Reads verse 2b.

Reader 1: Reads verse 3.

Reader 2/Congregation: Reads verses 4–5.

Reader 1: Reads verse 6.

Reader 2/Congregation: Reads verses 7–8.

Reader 1: Reads verse 9.

Reader 2/Congregation: Reads verse 10.

Reader 1: Reads verse 11.

Reader 2/Congregation: Reads verses 12–13, 17.

All: Read verse 18.

Gospel

Matthew 28:1–10

The Night is over. The Day has come.
It's dawn.
The first day of the week.
The Sabbath has passed.
And Mary and Mary
Are back at the tomb.

The Night is over. The Day has come.
There is an earthquake.
And an angel.
Who rolls away the stone
In front of the tomb
And then sits himself down on it.
He is bright as lightning,
As white as snow.
And the soldiers tremble
And the soldiers faint
When they see him.

The Night is over. The Day has come.
The angel speaks to the women.
"Don't be afraid.
I know who you're looking for.
Jesus, who was crucified
But he is not here.
He has risen
Just as he said."

The Night is over. The Day has come.
"Come see for yourself,"
The angel continues.

"See the place where he lay.
Then go
And tell his disciples.
He has risen
And will meet them in Galilee."

The Night is over. The Day has come.
The women leave the tomb
Filled with fear
Filled with joy
And then, suddenly,
There is Jesus.
"Greetings," he says
(As if it's just an ordinary day),
But Mary and Mary fall to their knees
Clasp his feet
And worship him.

The Night is over. The Day has come.
"Don't be afraid," says Jesus.
"Galilee,
That's where my brothers need to go.
Tell them they will see me there."

The Night is over. The Day has come.
Jesus is alive.

EASTER DAY

First reading

Acts 10:34–43

Reader 1: God doesn't play favourites. He accepts people from EVERY nation who fear him and do the right thing. Everyone.

Reader 2: Fair enough, he sent the message, first of all, to Israel, his chosen people.

But the message was a message of PEACE. Peace with God. Peace among people.

That message came through Jesus, who is Lord of ALL.

He was anointed with the Holy Spirit and Power. He did good. He healed all who were under the devil's power. And he did it because God was with him.

Reader 3: We saw what happened.

He was crucified, he was raised on the third day.

And he made sure he was seen, not by everybody, mind you, but by chosen witnesses, who ate and drank with him.

Reader 4: And this is what he asked the witnesses to do.

To preach to people.

To testify that Jesus is the one God appointed as judge of the living and the dead.

To follow the lead of the prophets who testified about him.

And to join them in making it clear that EVERYONE who believes in him will have their sins forgiven in his name.

I'll say it again (why don't you say it with me) – EVERYONE!

Gospel

John 20:1–18

I thought it might be nice to have some visual symbols to help you work through this story. They could be placed on a table at the front by the reader (or perhaps a different reader for each section) or by a helper.

This is followed by an alternative version which combines the use of visual "props" with the Bible text (ignoring my retelling completely).

The story begins with a stone. *(Place a stone on the table. Should you want to make a full-size papier maché replica you can omit the next line.)*

A stone much bigger than this one!

It's the first day of the week. It's still dark. And Mary Magdalene goes to Jesus' tomb and discovers that the stone in front of the tomb has been moved away.

So she runs as fast as she can to find Peter and John. And, breathless, she tells them the news.

"Somebody has taken the Lord from his tomb. I have no idea where they have put him."

The story continues with strips of linen. *(Place long strips of white cloth on the table.)*

Peter and John take off for the tomb. John is faster. He gets there first. And like a disciple-detective, he examines the scene. And peeping into the tomb, he finds strips of linen.

Next there is a folded cloth. *(Place a folded cloth on the table.)*

Peter catches up and goes straight inside. He sees the strips of linen, too. And the burial cloth that would have been wrapped round Jesus' head. But it's just lying there, folded neatly.

John finally goes in, too. And when he sees what's there, he believes that Jesus is alive. *(Until then, neither he nor Peter had understood from the Scriptures that Jesus would need to rise from the dead.)*

And then there are tears. *(Place a box of tissues on the table.)*

The disciples go back home, but Mary returns to the tomb. And there she stands, crying. As she weeps, however, she bends down to look inside. And what she sees is even more amazing than the sight that greeted the disciples.

Two angels are seated where Jesus' body had been laid – one at the place where his head had been, the other at the foot.

"Why are you crying?" they ask her.

"Because someone has taken my Lord away," she says. "And I have no idea where they have put him."

And that's when a gardener appears. *(Place some garden hand tools on the table – or flowers – whatever you think works best.)*

Or at least that's who Mary thinks it is. It's Jesus, actually, but she doesn't realize it.

He asks the same question as the angels.

"Why are you crying?" And then, "Who are you looking for?"

"If you have taken him," Mary begs. "Tell me where he is, please. And I will go and get him!"

And then the gardener says her name.

"Mary."

And a cry bursts forth from her that echoes round the garden. That echoes through the years. That echoes here in this place, now.

"*Rabboni!* Teacher!"

But when she reaches out for him, he says: "Don't hold onto me. I haven't yet returned to my Father. Instead, go tell my brothers that I am returning to our Father and to our God."

And then there is news to tell. *(Place a newspaper on the table.)*

So Mary goes to the disciples and tells them all that has happened. And the headline is simply this:

"I have seen the Lord," she says.

"I have seen the Lord!"

Alternative version

The items are brought to the front as the following verses are read.

Verses 1–2: Stone

Verses 3–5: Linen Strips

Verses 6–9: Cloth

Verses 10–13: Tissues

Verses 14–17: Garden tools/flowers

Verse 18: Newspaper

THE SECOND SUNDAY OF EASTER

First reading

Acts 2:14a, 22–32

You will need two readers for this piece.

Reader 1: Jesus of Nazareth came from God.

Reader 2: He performed miracles, wonders and signs through God.

Reader 1: And you know this because you were there.

Reader 2: And what was your response? You put him to death.

Reader 1: Okay, it was in God's plan that it happened.

Reader 2: But you still need to take the blame for nailing him to the cross. You and other wicked men.

Reader 1: So what did God do? He raised Jesus from the dead, that's what.

Reader 2: He freed him from death's agony, because it was beyond death's power to hold him.

Reader 1: You don't believe me? Here's what David said:

Reader 2: Reads Psalm 16:8–11a

Reader 1: And before you tell me that David said this about himself, let me remind you of a few things.

Reader 2: David died and was buried. And I can show you his tomb.

Reader 1: But he was also a prophet who believed God's promise that one of his descendants would sit on his throne.

Reader 2: So in this passage he speaks not of himself.

Reader 1: But looks forward to the resurrection of the Messiah.

Reader 2: Thus it is the Messiah who is not "abandoned to the grave".

Reader 1: It is the Messiah whose body does not "decay".

Reader 2: It is Jesus, whom God has raised to life.

Both Readers: The risen Jesus, whom we have seen!

Gospel
....

John 20:19–31

Jesus is alive.
It's evening, the first day of the week,
And the disciples are together,
Behind locked doors;
Still in fear of the Jewish leaders.

Jesus is alive.
And they know it
Because, suddenly, there he is
Standing among them!
"Shalom," he says.
Just an ordinary greeting.
But there's nothing ordinary about this moment,
As he shows them his hands and his side.
The disciples are overjoyed.

Jesus is alive.
"Shalom," he says again.
"Peace be with you."
And then he gives them a job.
"My Father sent me," he says.
"Now I am sending you."
And he gives them what they need for the job
By breathing on them.
"Receive the Holy Spirit," he says.
"What you forgive is forgiven;
What you don't forgive is not."
And then he goes.

Jesus is alive.
The disciples have seen him.
Well, all the disciples bar one.
Thomas is his name.
And when the others tell him what happened
He is incredulous
(A much bigger word than "doubting",
which means much the same thing.)
And before you start casting aspersions
And placing adjectives before his name
Consider, for a moment, how you might have reacted
Had you, alone among your mates,
Missed the most amazing thing that was ever likely to happen to you.
"You say you saw the nail marks in his hands?"
Thomas asks.
"You say you saw his wounded side?
Well, until I put my fingers in those nail marks,
Until I put my hand into his side,
I will not believe."

Jesus is alive.
A week has passed.
The disciples are together again.
And this time, Thomas is there, too.
The doors are still locked.
But locks don't keep Jesus from
Suddenly standing among them again.
Jesus greets them, "Shalom."
And then he turns to Thomas
And holds out his hands.
"Put your finger here," he says.
"And put your hand into my side.
Don't doubt. Believe!"
But, instead of reaching out his finger
or his hand,
Thomas simply opens his mouth.
"My Lord and my God," he confesses.

Jesus is alive
"You have seen me," he says.
"And because of that, you have believed."
"Blessed are those," he continues.
"Who believe without seeing."
And that's why this book has been written.
John concludes.
Not to tell everything that Jesus did.
But to tell enough that you might believe
That Jesus is the Christ, the Son of God,
And that by believing you might have life in his name.

Because Jesus is alive.

THE THIRD SUNDAY OF EASTER

First reading

Acts 2:14, 36–41

You will need to tell the congregation that they should repeat the reader's action and last line of each verse. You might need a second person to lead them in that.

Reader: So Peter stood up before he crowd
The other eleven were with him
"Fellow Jews," he said. "Residents of Jerusalem.
"Listen to what I have to say." *(Put hand to ear)*

Congregation: "Listen to what I have to say." *(Put hand to ear)*

Reader: Then he told them about Jesus
And finished by saying
"Be sure of this, Israel.
"God made Jesus both Lord and Christ
"That's right, the one you crucified." *(Make shape of cross with fingers)*

Congregation: "That's right, the one you crucified." *(Make shape of cross with fingers)*

Reader: When the people heard this
They were devastated,
Mortified,
Cut to the heart.
So they said to Peter and the apostles
"What should we do?" *(Hold out hands, palms up)*

Congregation: "What should we do?" *(Hold out hands, palms up)*

Reader: "Repent," said Peter.
"Be baptised," said Peter.
"In the name of Jesus, for the forgiveness of your sins.
"And you will receive his Holy Spirit, too.

"You and your children, and even those far off.
"All He chooses to call." *(Hand to mouth, as if calling)*

Congregation: "All He chooses to call." *(Hand to mouth, as if calling)*

Reader: Peter warned them
And he pleaded with them
To save themselves from their corrupt generation
And many believed what he said.
And many were baptised
Three thousand people in all. *(Hold three fingers in air)*

Congregation: Three thousand people in all. *(Hold three fingers in air)*

Gospel
....

Luke 24:13–35

> Jesus is alive
> *It's the first day of the week*
> *Two of his disciples are on the road*
> *From Jerusalem to Emmaus*
> *A seven-mile walk*
>
> Jesus is alive
> *That's what they're talking about*
> *The news they'd heard that morning*
> *From the women*
> *Who'd been to the empty tomb*
>
> Jesus is alive
> *And so he joins them*
> *Along the road*
> *Just like that*
> *But they are kept*
> *From recognizing him*

Jesus is alive
And he asks them
"What are you talking about?"
So they stop, shocked
And one of the disciples,

Cleopas, says
"You must be the only visitor
to Jerusalem
Who doesn't know
What has happened
These last few days!'

Jesus is alive.
"So tell me," he says.
And Cleopas does.
"Jesus of Nazareth," he says
"Was a prophet who did amazing things.
We thought he was The One
The Messiah
God promised to send
To save his people
But three days ago,
The chief priests had him crucified
And then, this morning,

Some of our women friends
Went to his tomb
His body was gone
But there were angels there
Who told them that he was alive.
Then some of our other friends
Went to the tomb, as well
And found it empty,
Just as the women had said."

Jesus is alive
So he responds to Cleopas.
And he's pretty blunt.
"You're foolish," he says
"And slow to pick up on
What the prophets
Have said, time and again,
About the Messiah:
That he was supposed to suffer
Before he entered into his glory."
Then, starting with Moses,
He leads Cleopas and his mate
On a journey through what
All the prophets had to say
About the Christ.

Jesus is alive
It's getting dark
And he finally arrives at Emmaus
With Cleopas and his mate
He acts like he wants to go further
But Cleopas convinces him
To stop for the night
They sit down to eat
Jesus takes bread
He gives thanks
He breaks it
And suddenly,
Cleopas and his mate
Know exactly who's sitting with them!

Jesus is alive
And just as suddenly
He disappears,

Cleopas and his mate
look at one another, amazed.

"Were our hearts not burning,"
they say,
"When he walked with us
And talked about the Scriptures?"

Jesus is alive
So they leg it
back to Jerusalem
All seven miles
And what do they find?
Jesus has appeared to Peter, as well
So they tell the eleven what happened to them
When Jesus walked with them
And talked with them
And how they knew it,
When he broke the bread,
That Jesus was with them
And Jesus is alive!

THE FOURTH SUNDAY OF EASTER

First reading

Acts 2:42–47

This is a snapshot of the life of the early church, so why not take a few pictures? There are bound to be plenty of phone cameras in your congregation, so have everyone take out their phones and turn them on (that announcement will come as a bit of a suprise) and make sure that the "flash" is on, as well. Tell them that, whenever you say "Flash!" they are to snap a picture of someone, and then read the line on the screen at the front. The reader then follows with his line or lines.

Reader: The believers devoted themselves… Flash *(flash)*

Congregation: To the apostles' teaching and to fellowship, to the breaking of bread and to prayer.

Reader: Everyone was filled with awe… Flash *(flash)*

Congregation: At the many wonders and signs performed by the apostles.

Reader: All the believers were together… Flash *(flash)*

Congregation: And had everything in common.

Reader: They sold property and possessions… Flash *(flash)*

Congregation: To give to anyone who had need.

Reader: Every day… Flash *(flash)*

Congregation: They continued to meet together in the temple courts.

Reader: They broke bread in their homes… Flash *(flash)*

Congregation: And ate together with glad and sincere hearts…

Reader: Praising God and enjoying the favour of all the people… Flash *(flash)*

Congregation: And the Lord added to their number daily those who were being saved.

Gospel

. . . .

John 10:1–10

This reading is pretty simple. The reader reads each section, and the congregation repeats what she says at the end of the "And all of the people said…" lines.

So, for example, at the end of the first section, the people would say "Baa" after the reader does. It might be helpful to explain this and do a practice line before you begin.

"I've got something to say about sheep," said Jesus.
And all of the people said, "Baaa."

"Let's start with the sheep thief," said Jesus. "That rotten, no-good, rustler."
And all of the people said, "Booo!"

"How does the sheep thief get into the pen?" asked Jesus. "Not through the gate, that's for sure. He creeps over the wall, in the dead of night, when nobody else is looking."
And all of the people said, "Sneaky!"

"And what is he there for?" asked Jesus. "I'll tell you – he's up to no good. He has knives and shears and lashings of mint sauce. He comes to steal and to kill and to destroy."
And all of the people said, "Nasty!"

"But the shepherd," said Jesus, "the shepherd is different."
And all of the people asked "How?"

"He comes through the gate," said Jesus. "The right way. The proper way. The honest way. And he comes not to kill, but to lead the sheep to pastures green and gently flowing waters."
And all of the people said, "Lovely!"

"I am the Gate of the sheep pen," said Jesus.
And all of the people said, "Huh?"

"I am the Gate!" said Jesus. "I'll protect you from anything and anyone that sneaks in to steal your joy. And if you go through me, you'll find life and find it to the full."

THE FIFTH SUNDAY OF EASTER

First reading

Acts 7:55–60

You could do this in a number of ways. You could have one reader, who simply points to her eyes, ears, etc. as she reads the passage. You could have a helper for the reader who leads the congregation in pointing to the different body parts. You could have the congregation repeat and point after the reader.

EYES

Filled with the Holy Spirit, Stephen looked up to heaven.
"Look," he said. "I see the Son of Man, standing at God's right hand."

EARS

When they heard what to them was blasphemy, Stephen's killers covered their ears.

MOUTHS

Then they yelled at the tops of their voices.

HANDS

And they grabbed hold of him and dragged him out of the city.
And they grabbed hold of rocks and began to stone him.

FEET

And they laid their clothes at the feet of a young man called Saul.

KNEES

But as the stones struck, sharp and hard and fast, Stephen cried, "Lord Jesus, receive my spirit."
Then, falling to his knees, he added, "Do not hold this sin against them."
Then he shut his eyes, and he died.

EYES

Second reading

1 Peter 2:2–10

You will need two readers – one to read the Scripture passage (in italic), the other to read the "choosy" comments. Feel free to replace my "choosiness" with "choosiness" of your own – to make it more specific to your needs!

Like newborn babies, crave pure spiritual milk, so that by it you may grow up in your salvation, now that you have tasted that the Lord is good.

As you come to him, the living Stone – rejected by humans but chosen by God and precious to him – you also, like living stones, are being built into a spiritual house to be a holy priesthood, offering spiritual sacrifices acceptable to God through Jesus Christ. For in Scripture it says:

"See, I lay a stone in Zion,

a chosen and precious cornerstone,

and the one who trusts in him

will never be put to shame."

Now to you who believe, this stone is precious. But to those who do not believe,

"The stone the builders rejected

has become the cornerstone,"

and,

"A stone that causes people to stumble

and a rock that makes them fall."

They stumble because they disobey the message—which is also what they were destined for.

But you are a chosen people, a royal priesthood, a holy nation, a people belonging to God, that you may declare the praises of him who called you out of darkness into his wonderful light.

When we first moved to town, we had a pretty clear idea of the kind of church we were looking for. The worship had to be right, for a start.

But you are a chosen people, a royal priesthood, a holy nation, a people belonging to God.

Post-Kendrick. Pre-Redman. That's what we had in mind. And we thought we'd found it. But when the organist at the first church we joined played the chorus of "Shine, Jesus, shine" while the offering was being collected; we knew right then and there that the Lord was telling us to leave.

That you may declare the praises of him who called you out of darkness into his wonderful light.

The next church was better. Yes, they seemed to love God and love one another. But they weren't really in touch with the Spirit. They weren't "moving on" – if you know what I mean.

But you are a royal priesthood, a holy nation.

So we tried a church on the other side of town. Sadly, the pastor was entirely too legalistic. He wouldn't let women pray!

A holy nation, a people belonging to God.

While the pastor at the next place was entirely too loose. He wanted women to preach!

That you may declare the praises of him.

So God called us on. What could we do?

Who called you out of darkness into his wonderful light.

But everywhere we went it was the same story.

But you are a chosen people

The paintwork was too bright.

A royal priesthood

The drums were too loud.

A holy nation

The incense made me sneeze.

A people belonging to God

The woman sitting next to me had a funny nose.

That you may declare the praises of him who called you out of darkness into his wonderful light.

I think the church is like a supermarket! If you don't like the quality of the produce at Tesco's, you can always pop down to Sainsbury's. Or Asda. Or even the corner shop. Choice – that's the important thing. Keeping the customer satisfied. And I'm sure that's true of church, as well.

But you are a chosen people.

THE SIXTH SUNDAY OF EASTER

First reading

Acts 17:22–31

This is a two-hander. One person should read the Bible text (italic type) while someone else does the rest. This story works best if the Bible readings and story parts flow as seamlessly as possible together.

So Paul waltzed into Athens with a tune on his lips. It was a gospel tune – "Jesus is the Answer" by Andraé Crouch (or was it The Jesse Dixon Singers?). In any case, it had played well in Derbe and Lystra and Antioch, and even in that "prison ministry" thing he'd stumbled into at Philippi. But would it play well here? In Athens? The first signs were not encouraging.

While Paul was waiting in Athens, he was greatly distressed to see that the city was full of idols."

So he decided to start with an audience who was at least a little familiar with his tune.

So he reasoned in the synagogue with the Jews and the God-fearing Greeks, as well as in the marketplace day by day with those who happened to be there.

And that's where he ran into a crowd who knew an entirely different set of songs.

A group of Epicurean and Stoic philosophers began to dispute with him. Some of them asked, "What is this babbler trying to say?" Others remarked, "He seems to be advocating foreign gods."

The Stoics were playing some sophisticated stuff – a bit of classical, a bit of jazz, the Blue Nile's "Downtown Lights". But the Epicureans – all they wanted to do was dance! Soul, funk, hip-hop, house – there was always some sort of party going on. And that wasn't all – Athens was buzzing with every other musical style. Heavy metal, alt-country, blues, punk, gangsta rap. How was Paul ever going to get heard in the midst of all this sound? As it happens, however, the Athenians were an eclectic bunch. Or maybe they were just on the lookout for the Next Big Thing.

Then they took him and brought him to a meeting of the Areopagus, where they said to him, "May we know what this new teaching is that you are presenting? You are bringing some strange ideas to our ears, and we want to know what they mean." (All the Athenians and the foreigners who lived there spent their time doing nothing but talking about and listening to the latest ideas.)

Paul wanted to sing his song, he really did. But it occurred to him that it might be helpful for his audience to know that he understood and appreciated their stuff, too. So he took a chance and launched into a tune that had echoes of gospel, but a bit of what turned them on, as well.

Paul then stood up... and said: "Men of Athens! I see that in every way you are very religious. For as I walked around and looked carefully at your objects of worship, I even found an altar with this inscription: TO AN UNKNOWN GOD."

Then he tried a bit of U2 with them, to help them to see that they still hadn't found what they were looking for. They liked the song. They really did. The Athenians were tapping their toes and nodding their heads. Some of them were even mouthing the words and doing that "Edge" thing on their air guitars. So Paul decided to shift gears and work a little of his own tune into the mix.

"Now what you worship as something unknown I am going to proclaim to you. The God who made the world and everything in it is the Lord of heaven and earth and does not live in temples built by hands. And he is not served by human hands, as if he needed anything, because he himself gives all men life and breath and everything else. From one man he made every nation of men, that they should inhabit the whole earth; and he determined the times set for them and the exact places where they should live. God did this so that men would seek him and perhaps reach out for him and find him, though he is not far from each one of us."

Most of the crowd was still swaying, still moving to Paul's groove. But some on the fringes were losing interest – chatting with their girlfriends, jabbering into their mobile phones. So Paul thought it might be time to switch gears again. He took a chance, a big chance for a rich boy from the posh end of

Tarsus – and he broke into a rap. But he was clever, Paul was, and he lifted his lyrics from some of Athens' best – Dirty Ol' Epimenedes the Cretan and DJ Dizzy Aratus.

"For in him we live and move and have our being. As some of your own poets have said, 'We are his offspring.'"

The crowd was with him again, so Paul decided to segue back into his original tune. He took a deep breath and gave it everything he had. He was Marvin Gaye looking for sexual healing. He was Aretha just looking for respect. He was Van the Man looking down at the crowd at the Rainbow Theatre and shouting out that it was simply too late to stop now!

"Therefore since we are God's offspring, we should not think that the divine being is like gold or silver or stone – an image made by man's design and skill. In the past God overlooked such ignorance, but now he commands all people everywhere to repent. For he has set a day when he will judge the world with justice by the man he has appointed. He has given proof of this to all men by raising him from the dead."

And then, suddenly, Paul felt like a dead man, too. He was Dylan on his English tour in the summer of '66, and even though no one shouted out "Judas" (largely because he hadn't actually yet told them who Judas was!), the feeling was much the same. The crowd turned on him. Some of them sneered, some of them booed and most of them walked out of the show. But there were a few, just a few, who came up to him after the show was over, their autograph books in their hands.

"We want to hear you again on this subject," they said.

And there were others, who even started singing Paul's song.

A few men became followers of Paul and believed. Among them was Dionysius, a member of the Areopagus, also a woman named Damaris, and a number of others.

So Paul waltzed out of Athens, still humming his tune. And even though they weren't quite yet Andraé Crouch or even The Jesse Dixon Singers, he managed to leave his own little gospel choir behind.

Gospel
....

John 14:15–21

You will need two readers – one to introduce each section and lead the congregation in the actions (the reader does the action, the congregation repeats it), and the other to read the passage.

Reader 1: What are Jesus' goodbye promises about? They're about love (*hand on heart*) and obedience (*salute*). *(Each reader demonstrating one action.)*

Reader 2: Reads verse 15.

Reader 1: They're about a gift (*reach out hands as if giving something away*) – the gift of the Spirit (*blow*).

Reader 2: Reads verses 16–17.

Reader 1: They're about not being orphans *(hold pretend bowl – can I have some more, please).*

Reader 2: Reads 18–19a.

Reader 1: And they're about life *(throw arms in air and shout "Life!")* and relationship *(put arm around someone).*

Reader 2: Reads verses 19b–20.

Reader 1: And just so we don't forget, they are about love (*hand on heart*) and obedience (*salute*).

Reader 2: reads verse 21.

ASCENSION DAY

First reading

Acts 1:1–11

There are four positions in this reading, so the congregation needs to stand while it's being read, and the reader needs to tell the congregation which position to take before he reads the corresponding section. It will help to explain this first, and it may even help to practise the positions.

Reader: The first part of our passage looks back, so turn around and look back.
Reads verses 1–3.

Reader: The second part of our passage is all about waiting – so cross your arms, or look at your wristwatch, as if you're standing and waiting for a bus or a train.
Reads verses 4–5.

Reader: The third part of our passage is about the ends of the earth, so put your hand over your eyes and peer off into the distance – as if you're looking a long, long way.
Reads verses 6–8.

Reader: And the final part of our passage is about looking up. So look up.
Reads verses 9–11.

Psalm

Psalm 47

This psalm offers several different opportunities for congregational responses which I think you should take advantage of. In fact, this psalm would work best woven into your sung worship. All you need is a reader and someone (your worship leader, possibly) to lead the congregation in their responses – you do need to leave space for the reading to be heard. I have long believed that the separation between sung worship and read/spoken worship in many churches has been a mistake, and a misunderstanding of the nature and breadth of worship itself. This psalm, rightly used, brings the sung and the spoken together – which is where they should be.

Reader: Reads verse 1a.

Congregation: Claps, applauds.

Reader: Reads verse 1b.

Congregation: Shouts for joy.

Reader: Reads verses 2–5a.

Congregation: Shouts again.

Reader: Reads verse 5b.

Congregation: Makes trumpet sounds – or if that seems to cheesy to you (which it can be!) perhaps the keyboard player makes a trumpet sound on keyboard – or maybe you have a trumpet in your band – which would, of course, work best of all!

Reader: Reads verse 6–7.

Congregation: Sings one or more songs of praise (specifically focused on God the King).

Reader: Concludes the time of worship and reads verses 8–9.

THE SEVENTH SUNDAY OF EASTER

Psalm

Psalm 68:1–10, 32–35

This reading breaks up nicely into four sections, each of which has four parts – an introductory thought, and three statements that (more or less) support it. So you will need one reader. And then I think it would be best to divide the congregation up into three groups, we'll call them A, B and C – to read the supporting statements – and to address them to one another, inasmuch as that is possible, given the design of your worship area.

Reader: Reads verse 1.

Group 1: Reads verse 2a.

Group 2: Reads verse 2b.

Group 3: Reads verse 3.

Reader: Reads verse 4.

Group 1: Reads verse 5.

Group 2: Reads verse 6 (ending at "singing").

Group 3: Reads rest of verse 6.

Reader: Reads verse 7.

Group 1: Reads verse 8.

Group 2: Reads verse 9.

Group 3: Reads verse 10.

Reader: Reads verse 32.

Group 1: Reads verse 33.

Group 2: Reads verse 34.

Group 3: Reads verse 35.

At the end of verse 35, everyone says together: "Praise be to God!"

Second reading

1 Peter 4:12–14; 5:6–11

This is one of those conversational responses to what Peter writes at the end of his first letter. You can either use two readers – one to read the text and the other to ask the questions/make the responses – or you can use a reader and the congregation.

Reader 1: Reads verse 12.

Reader 2/Congregation: "But we WERE surprised. We do think it's strange. And we're not sure how we should respond."

Reader 1: Reads verse 13a, ending with "…sufferings of Christ".

Reader 2/Congregation: "Rejoice? Really? Why?"

Reader 1: Reads verse 13b–14.

Reader 2/Congregation: "So we should rejoice in the midst of our suffering. Anything else we should do?"

Reader 1: Reads chapter 5, verse 6.

Reader 2/Congregation: "Okay. Fair enough. Things are tough, but we'll trust God and his timing."

Reader 1: Reads verse 7.

Reader 2/Congregation: "We'll do that, too. Anything else?"

Reader 1: Reads verse 8.

Reader 2/Congregation: "This we get. It feels like we're always under attack. So how do we deal with it?"

Reader 1: Reads verse 9.

Reader 2/Congregation: "So we're not alone. That's it, isn't it? God's with us. And our brothers, too. Do you think it will ever end? Do you think things will ever get better?"

Reader 1: Reads verses 10–11.

Reader 2/Congregation: "Amen to that. Amen."

DAY OF PENTECOST – WHIT SUNDAY

First reading

Acts 2:1–21

The actions for the chorus are included in the text. I think it's helpful to teach them before you tell the story, so everyone feels comfortable with what will happen.

> *Jesus' friends were watching and praying,*
> *Praying for the present that he had promised.*
> *Praying together in the city of Jerusalem.*
> *Praying on the Feast of Pentecost.*
>
> *Jesus' friends were watching and praying.*
> *When all of a sudden, their prayers were answered.*
> *They heard the roar of a rushing wind*
> *And tongues of fire licked their heads.*
>
> *Jesus' friends were watching and praying.*
> *When the Holy Spirit came upon them,*
> *Filled them, thrilled them, spilled right out of them*
> *With words they did not know.*

Chorus:
Make the wind blow (wave hands like wind)
Make the fire glow (make "flames" with fingers)
Take the words from your lips (pretend to touch God's lips)
And put them on our lips (touch own lips)
And speak them out to the whole of the world (make big ball/globe).

> *"What's going on?" asked the people of Jerusalem.*
> *"What can this possibly mean?*
> *These are plain Galileans, ordinary folk,*
> *Speaking words they never could have learned.*

"We come from the north, the south, and the east.
We come from all over the world!
Yet we all understand the things that they say
As they tell out the wonders of God."

Chorus

But some of the crowd were not so impressed.
Some even said they were drunk!
And that's when Peter, Jesus' friend,
Stood up and put them right.

"Filled with wine?" he said. "Not likely!
But we're filled with something else!
Filled with God's own Holy Spirit –
The power the prophets promised."

"And how did this happen?" asked Peter. "I'll tell you.
I'll tell you plain and true.
This is the gift of Jesus, the Messiah,
Whom you killed just six weeks ago!"

Chorus

The people were sorry, sad and ashamed.
And they cried, "What can we do?"
"Repent and be baptised," said Peter plainly.
And this gift will come to you!"

So the people repented, the people were baptised.
Three thousand people – or so!
And the word spread from there to the rest of Judea
And on to the rest of the world!

Chorus

Second reading
....

1 Corinthians 12:3b–13

This passage really lends itself to a call-and-response format, with one reader leading and the congregation responding, thus reinforcing the importance of the unity of the Body of Christ as expressed in this chapter.

Reader: No one can say, "Jesus is Lord," except by the Holy Spirit. There are different kinds of gifts,

Congregation: But the same Spirit distributes them.

Reader: There are different kinds of service,

Congregation: But the same Lord.

Reader: There are different kinds of working,

Congregation: But in all of them and in everyone it is the same God at work.

Reader: Now to each one the manifestation of the Spirit is given

Congregation: For the common good.

Reader: To one there is given through the Spirit

Congregation: A message of wisdom,

Reader: To another a message of knowledge

Congregation: By means of the same Spirit,

Reader: To another faith

Congregation: By the same Spirit,

Reader: To another gifts of healing

Congregation: By that one Spirit,

Reader: To another miraculous powers, to another prophecy, to another distinguishing between spirits, to another the speaking in different kinds of tongues, and to still another the interpretation of tongues.

Congregation: All these are the work of one and the same Spirit, and he distributes them to each one, just as he determines.

Reader: Just as a body, though one, has many parts,

Congregation: But all its many parts form one body, so it is with Christ.

Reader: For we were all baptised

Congregation: By one Spirit so as to form one body

Reader: – Whether Jews or Gentiles, slave or free –

Congregation: And we were all given the one Spirit to drink.

ORDINARY TIME

TRINITY SUNDAY

Psalm

Psalm 8

I think this psalm offers some lovely opportunities for interaction. I suggest you have a reader to read the passage and pause while the leader gives instructions and leads the congregation in their responses. If you have only one reader, she can still give directions in-between verses. I think this reading needs to be done with the congregation standing.

You could introduce the piece by telling everyone what they will be doing in each section, but I think it's more fun to just explain that you will be leading them in different responses, perhaps giving them one example, and then letting them enjoy the surprises along the way.

(Alternatively, after verse 1b, the leader's line could be: "Now let's hear from our children! I want all the kids to shout 'Hosanna, the Lord reigns' or 'God is good!'" Then the reader reads verse 2a – with a pause for the kids to shout – followed by verse 2b. Then resume at "Now let's look up at the sky.")

Leader: Let's all shout this together.

Reader: Reads verse 1a *(then everyone repeats)*.

Reader: Reads verse 1b.

Leader: Now let's look at our children. Look around if you have to. Lift them in the air if you can!

Reader: Reads verse 2 *(while everyone looks at the children)*.

Leader: Now let's look up at the sky *(everyone looks up)*.

Reader: Reads verses 3–4.

Leader: Now let's answer the question by looking at each other *(everyone looks at the person next to them).*

Reader: Reads verses 5–6.

Leader: Now let's make sheep and cow sounds.

Reader: Reads "all flocks and herds" *(everyone moos and baas).*

Leader: And let's make jungle animal sounds.

Reader: Reads "and the beasts of the field" *(everyone roars or screeches).*

Leader: And why not add a few bird sounds?

Reader: Reads "the birds of the air" *(everyone caws, tweets, and so on).*

Leader: And finally let's make some fishy movements.

Reader: Reads the rest of verse 8 *(while everyone makes fish, octopus, and dolphin motions).*

Leader: And let's finish where we started by shouting out the last line of the psalm.

Reader: Reads verse 9 *(everyone repeats).*

Gospel
....

Matthew 28:16–20

Reader 1: The story begins with a journey –

Reader 2: Eleven disciples go to Galilee.

Reader 1: It continues with a climb –

Reader 2: They ascend a mountain

Reader 1: And then there's a meeting.

Reader 2: Some are sure it's Jesus – so they worship him. Others aren't convinced.

Reader 1: So Jesus talks credentials.

Reader 2: "Authority in heaven? Authority on earth? It's all been given to me."

Reader 1: And having established that, he passes on his instructions.

Reader 2: Which can be summarized by the following verbs:

Reader 1: Go,

Reader 2: Go to all nations;

Reader 1: Make,

Reader 2: Make disciples;

Reader 1: Baptise

Reader 2: In the name of the Father, the Son, and the Holy Spirit.

Reader 1: Teach,

Reader 2: Teach them to obey;

Reader 1: Teach thoroughly

Reader 2: All that I have told you to do."

Reader 1: And finally there is a promise:

Reader 2: "I will be with you always."

Reader 1: A promise that lasts forever

Reader 2: To the very end of the age.

CORPUS CHRISTI

Second reading

1 Corinthians 11:23–26

You need two readers – one to lead the congregation in the actions, the other to read the passage.

Reader 1: It's about receiving *(grasp the air with both hands and pull arms into body)* and passing on *(extend arms and open hands).*

Congregation: Receiving *(repeat action)* and passing on *(repeat action).*

Reader 2: "For I received from the Lord what I also passed on to you."

Reader 1: It's about bread *(pretend to hold loaf in both hands)* and breaking *(pretend to break the loaf with both hands).*

Congregation: Bread *(repeat action)* and breaking *(repeat action).*

Reader 2: "The Lord Jesus, on the night he was betrayed, took bread, and when he had given thanks, he broke it and said,"

Reader 1: It's about eating *(put hand to mouth)* and remembering *(put finger to temple).*

Congregation: Eating *(repeat action)* and remembering *(repeat action).*

Reader 2: "'This is my body, which is for you; do this in remembrance of me.'"

Reader 1: It's about cups *(pretend to hold cup in air)* and covenants *(hand over heart).*

Congregation: Cups *(repeat action)* and covenants *(repeat action).*

Reader 2: "In the same way, after supper he took the cup, saying, 'This cup is the new covenant in my blood;'"

Reader 1: It's about drinking *(pretend to drink from cup)* and remembering *(put finger to temple).*

Congregation: Drinking *(repeat motion)* and remembering *(repeat motion)*.

Reader 2: "'Do this, whenever you drink it, in remembrance of me.'"

Reader 1: It's about eating *(repeat eating motion)* and drinking *(repeat drinking motion)* and proclaiming *(put hand to mouth and move outward from mouth)*.

Congregation: Eating *(repeat motion)* and drinking *(repeat motion)* and proclaiming *(repeat motion)*.

Reader 2: "For whenever you eat this bread and drink this cup, you proclaim the Lord's death until he comes."

Reader 1: It's about receiving *(repeat action)* and passing on *(repeat action)*.

Congregation: Receiving *(repeat motion)* and passing on *(repeat motion)*.

Gospel

John 6:51–58

You gotta think Manna.

"The living bread that came down from heaven?" said Jesus. "That's me. You eat of this bread you don't just live. You live forever. And what is this bread? It's my flesh, which I will sacrifice to bring life to the world."

You gotta stop thinking Cannibal.

The Jews argued among themselves: "What's he on about? How can he give us his flesh to eat?"

You gotta think Lifeblood.

"I'm only telling you what's true," said Jesus. "Unless you eat the flesh and drink the blood of the Son of Man, there's no life in you. But if you do eat my flesh and drink my blood, you have eternal life. And on the last day – I will raise you up. My flesh is genuine food. My blood is genuine drink."

You gotta think Intimacy.

"If you eat my flesh, if you drink my blood, then we are a part of each other.

It's like the relationship between me and my Father. He sent me. I live because of him. In the same way, the one who feeds on me will live because of me."

And then you gotta think Manna again. Manna Magnified. Manna Plus!

"This is what I mean when I talk about the bread that came down from heaven. Your ancestors ate manna, yes – and then they died. But if you eat of this bread, you will live forever."

PROPER 3

In some years the readings for Proper 3 will be used on the Sunday following Trinity Sunday. However, as this is more often used on the Third Sunday before Lent, the readings are to be found on page 58.

PROPER 4

First reading (Related)

Deuteronomy 11:18–21, 26–28

You will need one reader for Moses (more or less) and another person to lead the congregation in their words and actions (speaking for the people of Israel). The reading needs to start with everyone standing.

Reader 1: Moses called all Israel together. And this is what he told them: "Make sure that my words are fixed firmly in your hearts" *(put hand on heart)*.

Reader 2/Congregation: "In our hearts" *(repeat action)*.

Reader 1: "And in your heads" *(point to side of head)*.

Reader 2/Congregation: "And in our heads" *(repeat action)*.

Reader 1: "Tie them as symbols on your hands" *(pretend to wrap something round wrist)*.

Reader 2/Congregation: "On our hands" *(repeat action)*.

Reader 1: "Bind them on your foreheads" *(point to forehead)*.

Reader 2/Congregation: "On our foreheads" *(repeat action)*.

Reader 1: "Teach them to your children" *(look down and gesture in a teaching action – hold out hands, for example)*.

Reader 2/Congregation: "To our children" *(repeat action)*.

Reader 1: "Talk about them when you are sitting at home" *(sit down)*.

Reader 2/Congregation: "When we are sitting at home" *(repeat action)*.

Reader 1: "When you walk along the road" *(stand again and walk on the spot)*.

Reader 2/Congregation: "When we walk along the road" *(repeat action)*.

Reader 1: "When you lie down" *(sit again, but put hands behind head as if you are lying in bed).*

Reader 2/Congregation: "When we lie down" *(repeat action).*

Reader 1: "And when you get up again" *(stand up).*

Reader 2/Congregation: "And when we stand up" *(repeat action).*

Reader 1: "Write them on your door frames" *(pretend to reach up and write on door frame).*

Reader 2/Congregation: "On our door frames" *(repeat action).*

Reader 1: "And on your gates" *(reach down and pretend to write on gate).*

Reader 2/Congregation: "And on our gates" *(repeat action).*

Reader 1: "Do this and you will stay a long time in the land that God gave your ancestors – as long as the heaven *(look up)* is above the earth" *(look down).*

Reader 2/Congregation: "As long as the heaven *(look up)* is above the earth" *(look down).*

Reader 1: "You have a choice. One leads to blessing, the other to a curse. If you obey these commands, then you will receive a blessing."

Reader 2/Congregation: "A blessing" *(shout hooray!).*

Reader 1: "But if you disobey these commands and follow other gods, then you will receive a curse."

Reader 2/Congregation: "A curse" *(whisper "Oh dear").*

Psalm (Continuous)

Psalm 46

This works well as a call-and-response reading between one reader and the congregation.

Reader: Reads verse 1.

Congregation: Reads verses 2–3.

Reader: Reads verse 4.

Congregation: Reads verse 5.

Reader: Reads verse 6.

Congregation: Reads verse 7.

Reader: Reads verse 8.

Congregation: Reads verses 9–10.

All: Read verse 11.

PROPER 5

First reading (Continuous)

Genesis 12:1–9

You will need one reader to introduce each section and lead the congregation in the actions (see the words in italics); the other to read the rest of the text.

Reader 1: The story begins with a challenge, an offer, a proposition, a call *(hand to ear: "What's that?")*.

Reader 2: "Leave your country, your home, and your father," God says to Abram. "And go the place I will show you."

Reader 1: Next, there is a promise *(fingers crossed)*.

Reader 2: Well, several promises, actually:
"I will make you into a great nation," God says to Abram.
"I will bless you.
"Because of what I do through you, everyone will know your name.
"You will be a blessing.
"Anyone who blesses you, I will bless.
"Anyone who curses you will be cursed by me.
"And everyone on the earth will be blessed through you."

Reader 1: So Abram leaves *("I'm off!" Wave goodbye)*.

Reader 2: And he takes quite a crowd with him:
His wife, Sarah.
His nephew Lot.
All of their servants.
And all of their stuff.

And even though at seventy-five, he's not exactly a spring chicken, or even a summer chicken, or possibly not even an autumn chicken, Abram leads them all from Haran to the land of Canaan.

Reader 1: And when he arrives, he stops at a tree *(make a tree shape with arms)*.

Reader 2: The Great Tree of Moreh at Shechem, as it happens – a local beauty spot.

Abram notices (how can he help it?) that there are already people living in this place. Canaanites. So God appears to him and assures him that he will give this land to Abram's children. And in honour of this honour, Abram builds an altar near the tree.

Reader 1: And from there he scopes out the land *(hand over eyes – looking off into the distance – "Nice!")*.

Reader 2: He travels east of Bethel
And west of Ai
And sets up a tent.
And another altar.
And calls on the Lord.
Then heads off in the direction of the Negev.

Reader 1: Following his challenge, his offer, his proposition, his call *(hand to ear: "What's that?")*

Gospel
....

Matthew 9:9–13, 18–26

You will need one reader to introduce each section (generally just two words about Jesus) and lead the congregation in the actions and the other to read the rest of the text.

Reader 1: Jesus Looks.
(Congregation repeats line, hands over eyes.)

Reader 2: He sees a man called Matthew. A tax collector, sitting pretty in his tax collector's booth.
    "Come and follow me." says Jesus. And Matthew does.

Reader 1: Jesus Eats.
(Congregation repeats line and makes eating action.)

Reader 2: Matthew invites him home for dinner. And Jesus is not the only guest. Jesus' disciples are invited, too. Plenty of Matthew's tax collecting mates are there, as well, and other people who would have been called "sinners".

The Pharisees are not pleased with this arrangement and, rather than confronting Jesus, complain to his disciples: "Why does your teacher eat with these people? Tax collectors and sinners?"

Reader 1: Jesus Listens.
(Congregation repeats line, putting one hand to ear.)

Reader 2: It's not like he's hard of hearing. He knows what the Pharisees are saying about him.

"Healthy people don't need doctors," he says. "Sick people do.

"Seeing you're all so good at sorting out what God says is right and what's wrong, why not reflect on this Scripture?

"'I want mercy, not sacrifice.'

"That's why I have come, not to call the righteous, but the sinners."

Reader 1: Jesus Speaks.
(Congregation repeats line, pointing to mouth.)

Reader 2: And as he speaks, a ruler approaches him, falls on his knees, and begs Jesus for his help.

"My daughter has died. It just happened. But if you touch her with your hand she will live."

Reader 1: Jesus Goes.
(Congregation repeats line, making walking motion, swinging arms.)

Reader 2: He and his disciples leave with the man. But on the way, a woman who has suffered with bleeding for twelve years comes up from behind and touches his cloak – her thoughts a silent echo of the ruler's.

"If I can just touch his cloak, I'll be healed."

Reader 1: Jesus Turns.
(Congregation repeats line, each turning head or whole body, if standing.)

Reader 2: He sees her and his words are words of comfort.

"Take heart," he says.

"Your faith has healed you," he says.

And from that moment, she is well again.

Reader 1: Jesus Enters.
(Congregation repeats line and pretends to open door.)

Reader 2: He goes into the ruler's house and the mourners are already there – flutes playing, people wailing.

"Leave," he tells them.

"This girl isn't dead," he says. "She's just sleeping."

And the mocking laughter of the departing crowd can be heard right down the street.

But once they are gone, Jesus takes her by the hand. He touches her.

Reader 1: And when Jesus Looks
(Congregation repeats line and first action.)

Reader 2: She gets up out of her bed, alive!

And the news spreads throughout the land.

PROPER 6

First reading (Continuous)

Genesis 18:1–15 [21:1–7]

You will need one reader to introduce each section and lead the congregation in the actions (see the words in italics); the other to read the rest of the text.

Reader 1: The story begins with a tree
(make shape of tree with body and arms).

Reader 2: That's where God meets Abraham – at the Great Tree of Mamre. He comes as three men, and Abraham rushes from his tent and bows before them.

Reader 1: Next there is an invitation
(say "Répondez, s'il vous plait").

Reader 2: "Stay awhile," says Abraham. "Have your feet washed. Rest under this tree. Let me get you something to eat."

Reader 1: So bread is made
(pretend to knead dough).

Reader 2: Not by Abraham, mind you! All a flutter, he rushes into the tent, and asks his wife Sarah to whip up a loaf or two.

Reader 1: And cows are cooked
("Mooo!").

Reader 2: Not by Abraham, mind you! His wife is busy with the bread, so he runs to the herd and collects a calf and hands it to a servant to prepare.

Reader 1: And finally there is a meal
(pretend to eat, or say "MMMM!").

Reader 2: Once the bread is baked and the cow is cooked, Abraham delivers the lot (along with some milk and curds) to the three men under the tree.

Reader 1: And while they eat, they make a promise
(cross fingers).

Reader 2: "So where's your wife?" they ask.
"In the tent," Abraham gestures.
"Well, in a year's time," says the Lord, "I will return, and your wife will have a son."

Reader 1: And then there is a snigger
(all snigger)
And a giggle
(all giggle)
And a guffaw
(all laugh out loud).

Reader 2: It's coming from inside the tent.
It's coming from Sarah, who has been earwigging at the entrance.
It's coming from Sarah, who is well past childbearing age.
It's coming from Sarah, who says to herself.
"I'm worn out. My master is old. Will I really have this pleasure?"

Reader 1: So God repeats his promise
(two crossed fingers!).

Reader 2: "Why did Sarah laugh at what I said? Nothing is too hard for me. I'll come back in a year and, you'll see, Sarah will have a son."

Reader 1: And then Sarah is afraid
(trembling motion – say "Oh dear").

Reader 2: "I didn't laugh," she says.
"Oh yes you did!" says the Lord.

And then he is as good as his word.
In her old age, Sarah becomes pregnant.
In her old age, she gives birth to a son.
Abraham is a hundred years old when the boy is born.
And on the eighth day after his birth, Abraham circumcises him, as the Lord commanded.
And then he gives him a name.
A name that fits the promise and the circumstances of his birth. A name that

echoes the sound his wife made, hiding behind the tent flap.
He calls the boy Isaac.
A name that means laughter.

(All laugh!)

Psalm (Related)

Psalm 100

I see the possibility of using this psalm to frame a time of worship. You will need two readers, one to read the psalm, the other to lead the congregation in their response. At appropriate moments throughout the course of the psalm, there are opportunities for everyone to sing or pray.

Reader 1: "Shout for joy to the Lord, all the earth."

Reader 2/Congregation: We shout for joy *(and then shout!).*

Reader 1: "Serve the Lord with gladness;"

Reader 2/Congregation: We come before you, Lord, with gladness! *(make big smiles!).*

Reader 1: "Come before him with joyful songs."

Reader 2/Congregation: We come before you, Lord, with joyful songs!

At this point, everyone sings at least two (well, it is plural) joyful songs to the Lord. Afterwards, the reading continues more quietly, as follows:

Reader 1: "Know that the Lord is God."

Reader 2/Congregation: You are our God, Lord. We know that, even though we often try to take your place.

Reader 1: "It is he who made us, and we are his;"

Reader 2/Congregation: You made us. We belong to you.

Reader 1: "We are his people, the sheep of his pasture."

Reader 2/Congregation: We are your people, the sheep of your pasture.

At this point there are prayers thanking God for his sovereignty and provision, and asking for his help. A quiet song reflecting the theme of this section could be sung at the end of the prayers. Afterwards, the reading gets just that bit louder again, building to a crescendo.

Reader 1: "Enter his gates with thanksgiving…"

Reader 2/Congregation: And so we enter your gates with thanksgiving.

Reader 1: "And his courts with praise;"

Reader 2/Congregation: And we come into your courts with praise.

Reader 1: "Give thanks to him and praise his name."

Reader 2/Congregation: We thank you and we praise your name.

Reader 1: "For the Lord is good…"

Reader 2/Congregation: You are good, Lord!

Reader 1: "And his love endures forever;"

Reader 2/Congregation: You love us forever and ever.

Reader 1: "His faithfulness continues through all generations."

Reader 2/Congregation: And your faithfulness never ends! *(repeat 3 times)*.

End with another song or two of joyful praise reflecting God's enduring love!

PROPER 7

First reading (Related)

Jeremiah 20:7–13

The passage begins by showing Jeremiah in three different moods. So why not have three readers standing back to back in a kind of triangle shape, rotating so that the relevant reader faces the congregation? Then, after verse 10, have them stand in a row to deliver the final verses facing the congregation. I have suggested a simple action for each reader in the beginning section.

Reader 1 *(in accusatory tone)*: Reads verses 7–8 *(looking up, as if to God)*.

Reader 2: Reads verse 9 *(face down, hands clamped to chest, as if holding something)*.

Reader 3 *(in a loud whisper)*: Reads verse 10 *(one hand to mouth)*.

Following this, all face the congregation.

Reader 1: Reads verse 11, first sentence *(ending with "warrior")*.

Reader 2: Reads verse 11, second sentence *(ending with "prevail")*.

Reader 3: Reads the rest of verse 11.

Reader 1: Reads verse 12, first phrase *(ending with "mind")*.

Reader 2: Reads verse 12, first phrase *(ending with "them")*.

Reader 3: Reads rest of verse 12.

All readers together: Read verse 13.

Second reading

Romans 6:1b–11

You could use two readers for this one, to reflect the contrasts in the passage. Or you could use one reader and the congregation. I have also suggested some actions (in parentheses following some of the lines). Feel free to use, ignore, or alter these. If you do use them though, you might want someone to lead the congregation from the front, or put the instructions on a screen.

Reader 1: Shall we go on sinning so that grace may increase? *(Ask this like a real question, addressing the congregation or the other reader.)*

Reader 2/Congregation: By no means! *(Shouting this might be appropriate!)*

Reader 1: We are those who have died to sin; *(Extend hands to include all in the room.)*

Reader 2/Congregation: how can we live in it any longer? *(Look at one another as if asking those around you.)*

Reader 1: Or don't you know that all of us who were baptised into Christ Jesus were baptised into his death? *(Make a baptismal motion here – appropriate to your tradition.)*

Reader 2/Congregation: We were therefore buried with him through baptism into death *(baptismal motion again)*

Reader 1: in order that, just as Christ was raised from the dead through the glory of the Father, *(hands rising in air)*

Reader 2/Congregation: we too may live a new life *(another shout?)*.

Reader 1: For if we have been united with him in a death like his, *(arms wide, shape of cross)*

Reader 2/Congregation: we will certainly also be united with him in a resurrection like his *(arms raised)*.

Reader 1: For we know that our old self was crucified with him

Reader 2/Congregation: so that the body ruled by sin might be done away with, that we should no longer be slaves to sin *(pull apart hands like chains being broken)*.

Reader 1: Because anyone who has died

Reader 2/Congregation: has been set free from sin *(broken chains again)*.

Reader 1: Now if we died with Christ,

Reader 2/Congregation: we believe that we will also live with him. *(Again – look at each other as if confirming this truth among yourselves.)*

Reader 1: For we know that since Christ was raised from the dead,

Reader 2/Congregation: He cannot die again; death no longer has mastery over him *(shake head).*

Reader 1: The death he died, he died to sin once for all;

Reader 2/Congregation: But the life he lives, he lives to God *(point to sky).*

Reader 1: In the same way, count yourselves dead to sin

Reader 2/Congregation: But alive to God in Christ Jesus *(shout again?).*

PROPER 8

First reading (Continuous)

Genesis 22:1–14

You need two readers, one to introduce the passage and lead the congregation in their actions, and the other to read the story. This is a solemn story – so treat it solemnly.

Reader 1: Test (*pretend to answer exam question*). The story begins with a test.
(*Congregation repeats action.*)

Reader 2: "Abraham," says God. 'I want you to take Isaac. Isaac – your only son. Isaac – your beloved son. I want you to take Isaac up a mountain, up a mountain I will show you. And on that mountain, I want you to kill Isaac – to sacrifice him as a burnt offering."

Reader 1: Wood (*pretend to cut down tree*). The story continues with wood.
(*Congregation repeats action.*)

Reader 2: Abraham cuts wood. Wood enough for a burnt offering. He puts a saddle on his donkey. And with two of his servants and his only son Isaac, he sets off for the mountain. For three days they travel, and at last Abraham sees the place – away in the distance. So he tells his servants to wait while he and Isaac carry on together. He tells them that they will be worshipping the Lord. He tells them that they will return.

Reader 1: And then there is fire (*pretend to hold flaming torch – stare at it for a second as if watching the flames*). Abraham carries the fire.
(*Congregation repeats action.*)

Reader 2: Abraham carries the fire. And the knife. And the wood he gives to Isaac. Places it upon him.
     And as they walk together, Isaac asks a question. "We have fire and we have wood, Father. But where is the lamb for the offering?"
     And all the old man can say in reply is, "God will provide the lamb."

Reader 1: And now there is an altar (*pretend to lay one stone on another*).

Abraham builds an altar.
(Congregation repeats action.)

Reader 1: And then there is a rope *(pretend to tie a big knot)*. Abraham binds his son with a rope.
(Congregation repeats action.)

Reader 1: And out comes the knife *(pretend to hold knife in hand, then raise it)*. And as Abraham lays his son on the altar and raises the knife
(Congregation repeats action.)

Reader 2: An angel calls from heaven. "Abraham! Abraham!"
   "I am here," the old man replies.
   "Then do not harm the boy," says the angel. "Leave him alone. It is clear that you fear God – for you have not withheld even your only son."

Reader 1: Ram *(make twirly horn shape at side of head)*. And so there is a ram.
(Congregation repeats action.)

Reader 2: A ram caught by its horns in a thicket. So Abraham takes the ram and sacrifices it as a burnt offering in place of his son. And he names the place, as well – calls it "The Lord Will Provide". And so he did. And so the place is called to this day. "The Lord Will Provide." The Lord Will Provide – the sacrifice.

Second reading

Romans 6:12–23

Two readers are needed for this one, to reflect the contrasts in the passage. Or you could use one reader and the congregation. As in last week's passage from Romans, I have suggested some simple actions. Feel free to use, ignore, or alter these. Again, you might want someone to lead the congregation from the front, or put the instructions on a screen.

Reader 1: Therefore do not let sin reign in your mortal body so that you obey its evil desires. Do not offer any part of yourself to sin, as an instrument of wickedness,

Reader 2/Congregation: But rather offer yourselves to God, as those who have been brought from death to life; and offer the parts of your body to him as an instrument of righteousness.

Reader 1: For sin shall no longer be your master,

Reader 2/Congregation: Because you are not under the law, but under grace.

Reader 1: What then? Shall we sin because we are not under the law but under grace?

Reader 2/Congregation *(shout)***:** By no means!

Reader 1: Don't you know that when you offer yourselves to someone as obedient slaves, you are slaves of the one you obey – whether you are slaves to sin, which leads to death,

Reader 2/Congregation: Or to obedience, which leads to righteousness?

Reader 1: But thanks be to God that, though you used to be slaves to sin,

Reader 2/Congregation: You have come to obey from your heart the pattern of teaching that has now claimed your allegiance.

Reader 1: You have been set free from sin

Reader 2/Congregation: And have become slaves to righteousness.

Reader 1: I am using an example from everyday life because of your human limitations. Just as you used to offer yourselves as slaves to impurity and to ever-increasing wickedness,

Reader 2/Congregation: So now offer yourselves as slaves to righteousness leading to holiness.

Reader 1: When you were slaves to sin, you were free from the control of righteousness. What benefit did you reap at that time from the things you are now ashamed of? Those things result in death!

Reader 2/Congregation: But now that you have been set free from sin and have become slaves of God, the benefit you reap leads to holiness, and the result is eternal life.

Reader 1: For the wages of sin is death,

Reader 2/Congregation: But the gift of God is eternal life in Christ Jesus our Lord. *(Shout, perhaps cheer at end.)*

PROPER 9

Canticle (Continuous)

Song of Solomon 2:8–13

There is such a strong chance that using two readers (a man and a woman) here will lead to cheesiness, that I am reluctant to suggest it. And yet, it is such a beautiful passage, that, done right, it can really be incredible. Forgo any attempt at action (no leaping gazelles – unless what you are looking for is a parody version!). Perhaps it will work best if the woman is seated and the man stands. Keep it simple. Keep it serious. Let the words do their work.

Woman: Reads verses 8–10a.

Man: Reads verses 10b–13.

And if they can pull it off without it being cheesy, perhaps at the end he takes her by the hand, she rises, and they walk off together.

Second reading

Romans 7:15–25a

Using two readers to read Paul's words can really show the two sides at war within him and bring the familiar text to life in a new way. These words are from the NIV.

Both Readers: I do not understand what I do.

Reader 1: For what I want to do I do not do,

Reader 2: But what I hate I do. And if I do what I do not want to do, I agree that the law is good.

Reader 1: As it is, it is no longer I myself who do it,

Reader 2: But it is sin living in me. For I know that good itself does not dwell in me, that is, in my sinful nature.

Reader 1: For I have the desire to do what is good,

Reader 2: But I cannot carry it out.

Reader 1: For I do not do the good I want to do,

Reader 2: But the evil I do not want to do – this I keep on doing.

Reader 1: Now if I do what I do not want to do, it is no longer I who do it,

Reader 2: But it is sin living in me that does it.

Both Readers: So I find this law at work:

Reader 1: Although I want to do good,

Reader 2: Evil is right there with me.

Reader 1: For in my inner being I delight in God's law;

Reader 2: But I see another law at work in me, waging war against the law of my mind and making me a prisoner of the law of sin at work within me.

Reader 1: What a wretched man I am!

Reader 2: Who will rescue me from this body that is subject to death?

Both Readers: Thanks be to God – who delivers me through Jesus Christ our Lord!

PROPER 10

First reading (Continuous)

Genesis 25:19–34

Three readers are needed for this. One to narrate the first part of the text, and the other two for Jacob and Esau. These words are from the NIV.

Narrator: This is the account of the family line of Abraham's son Isaac.

Abraham became the father of Isaac, and Isaac was forty years old when he married Rebekah daughter of Bethuel the Aramean from Paddan Aram and sister of Laban the Aramean.

Isaac prayed to the Lord on behalf of his wife, because she was childless. The Lord answered his prayer, and his wife Rebekah became pregnant. The babies jostled each other within her, and she said, "Why is this happening to me?" So she went to inquire of the Lord.

The Lord said to her,

Jacob and Esau:
"Two nations are in your womb,
and two peoples from within you will be separated;
one people will be stronger than the other,
and the older will serve the younger."

Narrator: When the time came for her to give birth, there were twin boys in her womb.

Esau: The first to come out was red, and his whole body was like a hairy garment; so they named him Esau.

Jacob: After this, his brother came out, with his hand grasping Esau's heel; so he was named Jacob.

Narrator: Isaac was sixty years old when Rebekah gave birth to them.

Esau: The boys grew up, and Esau became a skilful hunter, a man of the open country…

Jacob: While Jacob was a quiet man, staying among the tents.

Esau: Isaac, who had a taste for wild game, loved Esau,

Jacob: But Rebekah loved Jacob.

Narrator: Once when Jacob was cooking some stew, Esau came in from the open country, famished.

Esau: He said to Jacob, "Quick, let me have some of that red stew! I'm famished!" (That is why he was also called Edom.)

Jacob: Jacob replied, "First sell me your birthright."

Esau: "Look, I am about to die," Esau said. "What good is the birthright to me?"

Jacob: But Jacob said, "Swear to me first."

Esau: So he swore an oath to him, selling his birthright to Jacob.

Jacob: Then Jacob gave Esau some bread and some lentil stew.

Esau: He ate and drank, and then got up and left.
So Esau despised his birthright.

Gospel
. . . .

Matthew 13:1–9, 18–23

The leader needs to teach the congregation three simple actions to do when the following words are said.

"So Go!" – stretch out right arms and point their finger as if to say "Go!"
"So Sow!' – stretch out left arms in a "sowing seeds" motion
"And Know" – point a finger to head or temple

> *So Go!*
> *So Sow!*
> *And Know*
> *The seeds you throw*
> *Are seeds not sown in vain.*

Yeah, some of them will fall along the path
Miss the soil altogether
And have no chance to hear
As Satan's sneaky sparrows steal them all away.
But others will land on the good earth
And seeds will sprout and buds will blossom
And fruit will weigh down branches
Thirty and sixty and a hundred times more!

So Go!
So Sow!
And Know
The seeds you throw
Are seeds not sown in vain.

And, yeah, some will fall on the rocky ground
Sink down and take root right away.
Till trouble comes like a scorching sun
And the soil is not deep enough
To save them from the withering day.
But others will land on the good earth
And vines will grow and wine will flow
And grapes will weigh down branches
Thirty and sixty and a hundred times more!

So Go!
So Sow!
And Know
The seeds you throw
Are seeds not sown in vain.

And, yeah, some will fall on the thorny ground
And the weeds of worry
And the weeds of wealth
Will strangle and shut out the light.

But others will land on the good earth
And rising right up to an elephant's eye
(or so the song says)
The corn will reach to the sky
Thirty and sixty and a hundred times high!

So Go!
So Sow!
And Know
The seeds you throw
Are seeds not sown in vain.

PROPER 11

Psalm (Continuous)

Psalm 139:1–12, 23–24

One reader leads the congregation. She does the action when she reads the words. The congregation says some of the words back (like an echo) and repeats the actions. The reading begins with everyone standing.

Reader: O Lord, you have searched me
and you know me.
You know when I sit *(sit)*

Congregation: When I sit *(repeat action)*

Reader: And when I rise *(stand back up again);*

Congregation: When I rise *(repeat action);*

Reader: You perceive my thoughts from afar.
You discern my going out *(pretend to open door)*

Congregation: My going out *(repeat action)*

Reader: And my lying down *(put hands behind head as if lying in bed);*

Congregation: My lying down *(repeat action);*

Reader: You are familiar with all my ways.
Before a word is on my tongue *(point to mouth)*

Congregation: On my tongue *(repeat action)*

Reader: You know it completely, O Lord.
You hem me in – behind *(look back)*

Congregation: behind *(repeat action)*

Reader: And before *(look forward again);*

Congregation: And before *(repeat action);*

Reader: You have laid your hand upon me *(stretch out hand).*

Congregation: Your hand upon me *(repeat action)*.

Reader: Such knowledge is too wonderful for me,
too lofty for me to attain.
Where can I go from your Spirit?
Where can I flee from your presence?
If I go up to the heavens *(reach hand up)*,

Congregation: Up to the heavens *(repeat action)*,

Reader: You are there;
If I make my bed in the depths *(reach down and pretend to straighten sheet)*,

Congregation: In the depths *(repeat action)*,

Reader: You are there.
If I rise on the wings of the dawn *(stretch arms to side like wings)*,

Congregation: If I rise on wings *(repeat action)*,

Reader: If I settle on the far side of the sea *(point off into the distance)*,

Congregation: the far side of the sea *(repeat action)*,

Reader: Even there your hand will guide me,
Your right hand will hold me fast.
If I say, "Surely the darkness will hide me *(put arms over face, as if hiding)*

Congregation: Hide me *(repeat action)*

Reader: And the light become night around me."

Even the darkness will not be dark to you;
the night will shine like the day,
for darkness is as light to you.

Search me, O God and know my heart *(hand over heart)*;

Congregation: Know my heart *(repeat action)*;

Reader: Test me and know my anxious thoughts *(point finger to head)*.

Congregation: My anxious thoughts *(repeat action)*.

Reader: See if there is any offensive way in me,
And lead me in the way everlasting *(stretch hand out as if showing the way)*.

Congregation: The way everlasting *(stretch hand out as if showing the way)*.

Gospel

. . . .

Matthew 13:24–30, 36–43

You will need someone to tell the story. You will also need to break the congregation into two groups. However, in order for the story to be effective, I suggest that you put everyone whose surname starts with A to M in one group, while the Ns to Zs are in the other. Unless your congregation seats themselves alphabetically, this should work well!

The A–M group will be the wheat/good seeds group. When they hear "wheat", you will lead them in saying (in a high and bright and happy voice) *"Good Seed – Wheat!"* The N–Z group will be the weeds. And when they hear "weeds", they will say (in a nasty voice) *"Bad Seed – Weeds"*.

Reader: Here is a parable Jesus told to the crowd:
"The kingdom of heaven is like a man who went to his field and sowed wheat *(Good Seed – Wheat!)*. But while he and his family and his workers were all sleeping, the man's enemy sneaked into the field and among the wheat *(Good Seed – Wheat!)* sowed weeds *(Bad Seed – Weeds!)*. And then he sneaked away, without anyone being the wiser.

But when the wheat *(Good Seed – Wheat!)* sprouted (you could gesture for them to stand at this point), the weeds *(Bad Seed – Weeds)* appeared, as well (also stand).

The servants of the man who owned the field came to him, confused. "We thought you sowed wheat *(Good Seed – Wheat!)*. Where did the weeds *(Bad Seed – Weeds)* come from?"

"This was the work of my enemy," the man said.

"Do you want us to pull them out?" the servants asked the man.

The man shook his head. "No. If you pull out the weeds *(Bad Seed – Weeds)*, you might also destroy the wheat *(Good Seed – Wheat!)*. Better to let them grow together, and then, when harvest comes, I'll tell the harvesters to gather up and bundle up and burn up the weeds (*Bad Seed – Weeds – sit them down again*). And then collect the wheat (*Good Seed – Wheat! – sit them down again*) and store it in my barn."

When Jesus had finished the parable, he left the crowd and went into a house. And that's where his disciples asked him to tell them the meaning of the parable.

And this is what Jesus said:

"The Son of Man is the person who sowed the wheat (*Good Seed – Wheat!).* The field is the world. And the good seed that produces the wheat (*Good Seed – Wheat!*) stands for the sons of the kingdom.

The weeds (*Bad Seed – Weeds!)* are the sons of the devil – and he is the enemy who sowed them in the field.

The Harvest is at the end of the age. And the angels are the harvesters.

And this is how it will be at the end of the age. The Son of Man will send his angels and they will pull up the weeds (*Bad Seed – Weeds*) from his kingdom – everything that causes sin and everyone who does evil. And then the angels will throw them into a fiery furnace – a place of weeping and gnashing of teeth.

But the righteous – the wheat (*Good Seed – Wheat!*) will shine like the sun in their Father's kingdom.

He who has ears, let him hear."

PROPER 12

First reading (Continuous)

Genesis 29:15–28

This retelling needs two readers. The first reader leads the congregation in echoing part of what he has just said.

Reader 1: The story begins with a labour negotiation *(shout "Show me the money!").*

Congregation: *(Shouts "Show me the Money!")*

Reader 2: "Yes, we're related," says Laban to Jacob. "But that doesn't mean you should work for me for nothing. Tell me, what sort of wages are you looking for?"

Reader 1: And that's where love enters the story *(say, slow and deep, Barry White style – with hand over heart – "Luuuurv!")*

Congregation: *(Repeats action and "Luuuurv".)*

Reader 2: Laban has two daughters. The older daughter, Leah, has weak eyes (depending on how you translate the passage – but the point is clear – she's by far the plainer of the two). But the younger daughter, Rachel, is a knockout! (And there is no mistaking the meaning here!) Jacob is in love with Rachel. And for his wages – for seven years' work – he asks for her hand in marriage.

Reader 1: And so, for the next seven years, Jacob works for his Uncle Laban. But he is so in love with Rachel that it hardly seems like any time at all *(count 1, 2, 3, 4, 5, 6, 7 – and then wipe forehead and say, "That wasn't too bad!").*

Congregation: *(Repeats counting and phrase.)*

Reader 2: "Right, then," says Jacob. "I've worked the seven years. I'd like my wife now."

So Laban throws a big party. He invites all the locals. Everyone eats till they are about to burst.

Reader 1: And that's when the story takes a turn – a nasty deceptive turn *(do an evil laugh – Nyah–ha–ha!)*.

Congregation: *(Repeats evil laugh.)*

Reader 2: When night falls, Laban sneaks Leah into Jacob's bed – instead of Rachel. He even gives her Zilpah, the younger of his two handmaidens, so that Jacob will think he is sleeping with Rachel.

So Jacob does just that – he sleeps with Leah.

Reader 1: And in the morning, when he discovers what has happened, he is gutted *(angry scream – AAAH!)*.

Congregation: *(Repeat angry scream.)*

Reader 2: "I did what you asked!'" Jacob protests. "I worked for Rachel for seven years. Why have you deceived me?"

"Ahhh," says Laban with a trickster's smile. "It's our custom here to marry the oldest daughter off before the younger. But I think we can come to an arrangement that will satisfy us both. Finish off the bridal week with Leah, promise me another seven years' of work, and you can have Rachel, too."

Reader 1: And that's when love kicks back in again *(repeat the "LUUURV" thing from above)*.

Congregation: *(Repeat the "LUUURV" thing.)*

Reader 2: Jacob accepts his uncle's offer. He finishes the bridal week with Leah. And then, at last, he takes Rachel to be his wife.

Gospel

Matthew 13:31–33, 44–52

Reader 1: "What's the kingdom of heaven like?" Jesus asked the crowd.

"It's like a mustard seed," said Jesus *(pretend to hold up a tiny seed between two fingers)*.

Congregation: A mustard seed *(repeats action)*.

Reader 2: And then he told them a parable:

"There once was a man who planted a mustard seed – planted it in his field. But even though it was the smallest of all the seeds, it grew into the biggest garden plant – big as a tree. Big enough for the birds to gather and perch on its branches."

Reader 1: "What's the kingdom of heaven like?" Jesus asked the crowd.
"It's like yeast," said Jesus *(make a kneading motion)*.

Congregation: Like yeast *(repeats action)*.

Reader 2: And then he told them a parable:
"There once was a woman making bread. She took just a little bit of yeast and she mixed it into a great big pile of flour. And it worked its way through all of the dough."

Reader 1: "What's the kingdom of heaven like?" Jesus asked the crowd.
"It's like treasure!" said Jesus *(pretend to open a treasure chest and go 'OOOOH!")*.

Congregation: Like treasure *(repeats action)*.

Reader 2: And then he told them a parable:
"There once was a man who found a treasure, hidden in a field. And what did he do? He hid that treasure. He joyfully sold everything he owned. And then he went and bought that field."

Reader 1: "What's the kingdom of heaven like?" Jesus asked the crowd.
"It's like a fine pearl" *(pretend to gaze at pearl in hand and say "Lovely!")*.

Congregation: Like a pearl *(repeats action)*.

Reader 2: And then he told them a parable:
"There once was a merchant, looking for fine pearls. And when he found an absolutely exquisite one – one of incredible value – he went away. He sold everything he had. And he bought that beautiful pearl."

Reader 1: "What's the kingdom of heaven like?" Jesus asked the crowd.
"It's like a net" *(pretend to type on computer)*.

Reader 2: What are you doing?

Reader 1: I'm pretending to go on the net. Why, should I have done the smartphone action *(pretend to trace finger on phone)*.

Reader 2: No, it's not that kind of net. It's a fishing net.

Reader 1: Ahhh, I see. Sorry. It's like a net *(do a casting net action)*.

Congregation: It's like a net *(repeat action – some smart alecks will, of course be typing)*.

Reader 2: And then he told them a parable:

"Once there was a fisherman who lowered his net into a lake. He caught all different kinds of fish. When the net was full, he pulled it out and set it on the shore and sorted through the fish. He kept the good ones and threw the bad ones away. And that's how it will be at the end of the age. Like the fisherman, the angels will sort through the wicked and the righteous. And the wicked will be thrown into the fiery furnace – a place of weeping and gnashing of teeth."

Reader 1: And then Jesus asked the crowd, "Do you understand what I'm saying?"

And the crowd nodded, "Yes" *(makes nodding motion)*.

Congregation: Yes *(nods as well)*.

Reader 1: "So what's a teacher of the law like?" Jesus asked the crowd, finally.

"He's like the owner of a house," said Jesus *(draw shape of house in air)*.

Congregation: The owner of a house *(repeats action)*.

Reader 2: And then – you guessed it! – he told them one last parable:

"Once there was an owner of a house. He went into his storeroom. And when he came out, he not only had old treasures, but new ones, too!"

PROPER 13

First reading (Continuous)

Genesis 32:22–31

This is an action story. So you will need one reader to describe the action and another reader to tell what the action accomplished.

Reader 1: Jacob rises.

Reader 2: It's night time. He wakes his two wives and his two maidservants and his eleven sons. There is somewhere they need to go.

Reader 1: Jacob crosses.

Reader 2: The ford of the river Jabbok. He leads his family across. He sends all his stuff as well. Then he returns, alone. But he is not alone for long.

Reader 1: Jacob wrestles.

Reader 2: A man appears, and Jacob wrestles with the man. All through what is left of the night. Up until the day breaks through the darkness.

Reader 1: Jacob endures.

Reader 2: Though he wrestles as hard as he can, the man does not overpower Jacob. So he touches the socket of Jacob's hip and it is wrenched out of place.
Then the man says, "Let me go. It's daybreak."

Reader 1: So Jacob bargains.

Reader 2: "I will only let you go if you bless me," Jacob says.
"Then what's your name?" asks the man.
And Jacob tells him.
"That may be so," the man says. "But from this moment on, your name will no longer be Jacob. You will be called Israel, for you have struggled with God and struggled with men and have overcome."

Reader 1: Then Jacob asks.

Reader 2: "What is *your* name?" he asks the man. And the man's only reply is "Why? Why do you ask my name?"

And then he gives Jacob his blessing.

Reader 1: So Jacob names.

Reader 2: He names the place where he wrestled. He calls it Peniel. For that is spot where he saw God face to face – and yet lived to tell the tale.

Reader 1: Then Jacob limps.

Reader 2: With the sun rising above him. With the start of a brand-new day. Jacob limps away from Peniel – a man with a brand new name.

Gospel
....

Matthew 14:13–21

Reader 1: Jesus is sad *(make sad face)*.

Congregation: Sad *(repeat action)*.

Reader 2: He hears that his cousin, John the Baptist, is dead. So he gets into a boat and sails away, to a private spot, to be alone.

Reader 1: But the crowds hear about it *(hand to ear)*.

Congregation: They hear about it *(repeat action)*.

Reader 2: So they come from all the towns nearby, come on foot to the spot where Jesus is going. And when he arrives he is far from alone – there are thousands and thousands of people waiting for him.

Reader 1: So Jesus has compassion on them *(put hand to heart)*.

Congregation: Compassion *(repeat action)*.

Reader 2: He heals their sick. He spends all day doing it. And when evening comes, his disciples suggest that it's time to send them away – so they can go to the villages and buy food.

Reader 1: But Jesus shakes his head *(shake head)*.

Congregation: He shakes his head *(repeat action)*.

Reader 2: "No," he says. "They don't need to go. You can feed them."
    And the disciples don't know whether to laugh or cry. "We only have two fish," they say. "And five loaves of bread!"
    "Then let me have them," Jesus says. "And tell the people to sit down on the grass."

Reader 1: So Jesus prays *(bow head, fold hands)*.

Congregation: He prays *(repeat action)*.

Reader 2: He gives thanks to God for the fish and the bread.

Reader 1: Then he breaks the bread *(pretend to break bread)*.

Congregation: Breaks it *(repeat action)*.

Reader 2: And he gives it to the disciples, who pass it round to the people.

Reader 1: And the people eat and are satisfied *(rub tummy or belch – or both!)*.

Congregation: They're satisfied *(repeat action)*.

Reader 2: And five thousand men are fed. And women and children, too. And there is so much food to go round, that the disciples fill twelve baskets with the leftovers!

PROPER 14

First reading (Continuous)

Genesis 37:1–4, 12–28

This is a Going Story. A To-ing and Fro-ing Story. Where God takes his people from a place where they will starve to a place where they will be safe. And this is how it starts:

Reader 1: Joseph goes to his father.

Reader 2: He's been out in the fields, tending the flocks with all his older brothers. And he goes to his father to rat on them – to tell Jacob that they haven't been tending all that well.

This only adds insult to injury, for the brothers all know that Joseph is Jacob's favourite son, born to him in his old age. And the brothers have all seen the beautiful, decorated robe that Jacob made for Joseph as a token of his love.

They hate their brother. It's as simple as that.

Reader 1: The brothers go to Shechem.

Reader 2: It's where they take the flocks to graze. And Jacob sends Joseph to meet them. To check up on them. To report back what he finds.

Reader 1: So Joseph goes to Shechem.

Reader 2: He travels from the Valley of Hebron, but when he gets to Shechem, his brothers are nowhere to be found. He meets a man and the man asks what he's looking for.

"My brothers," says Joseph.

And the man says:

Reader 1: "Your brothers have gone to Dothan."

Reader 2: So Joseph goes to Dothan. But when his brothers see him coming, they come up with a plan to bring his journey to a full and final end.

"Let's kill that dreamer," they say. "Let's dump his body in a cistern. Let's tell our father that an animal ate him. And we'll see what comes of his dreams!"

But one brother, Reuben, has a different idea. "Let's not shed any blood here. Let's throw him the cistern, fine. Let's teach him a lesson. But we shouldn't take his life."

Reuben hopes, you see, to return to the cistern later, to remove Joseph, and to take him safely back to his father.

Reader 1: So Joseph goes to his brothers.

Reader 2: And they set upon him. And they tear off his beautiful decorated robe. And they drag him to an empty cistern. And they dump him deep down inside.

Reader 1: The brothers go to eat their dinner.

Reader 2: And as they eat, a caravan of Ishmaelites, on their way from Gilead to Egypt, come "camelling" by. Their beasts are loaded with spices and balm and myrrh.

Reader 1: And as the Ishmaelites go by

Reader 2: Judah, one of the brothers, has an idea. "There's not much to be gained by just killing Joseph. Not much in it for us. But if we sell him to these Ishmaelites, we get rid of him, we keep our hands clean, and we make a tidy profit as well!"

Reader 1: So the brothers go the Ishmaelites

Reader 2: A bargain is struck. They sell their brother for twenty pieces of silver. The Ishmaelites pull him out of the cistern and lead him away.

Readers 1 and 2: And Joseph goes to Egypt.

Psalm (Continuous)

Psalm 105:1–6, 16–22, 45b

What I like about this psalm is its emphasis on what God has done – and its quick and powerful retelling of the Joseph story (among others) as an example of his mighty deeds. So the reading is designed to emphasize God's mighty acts.

Reader 1: Reads verse 1.

Congregation: Repeats the words "what he has done".

Reader 2: Reads verse 2.

Congregation: Repeats the words "his wonderful acts".

Reader 1: Reads verse 3.

Reader 2: Reads verse 4.

Reader 1: Read verse 5a.

Congregation: Repeats the words "he has done".

Reader 2: Reads verses 5a–6.

Readers 1 and 2: "And this is what he has done."

Reader 1: Reads verse 16.

Reader 2: Reads verse 17.

Reader 1: Reads verse 18.

Reader 2: Reads verse 19.

Reader 1: Reads verse 20.

Reader 1: Reads verse 21.

Reader 2: Reads verse 22.

Reader 1 and 2: "Praise the Lord."

Congregation: Repeats "Praise the Lord."

PROPER 15

First reading (Related)

Isaiah 56:1, 6–8

Two readers would be best for this one. You could even start with them on opposite sides of the building, gradually walking towards each other as verses 1, 6 and the first part of 7 are read. And once they are together, have them read the end of verse 7 in unison.

Reader 1: Reads verse 1.

Reader 2: Reads verse 6.

Reader 1: Reads verse, ending with "altar".

Both Readers: Read rest of verse 7.

Reader 2: Reads verse 8.

Gospel

Matthew 15:[10–20] 21–28

This is fine with one reader, but you might want to break it up with a second reader announcing just the "hard thing" lines and making a show of crossing them off an imaginary list.

Jesus says some hard things. Hard to understand. Hard to take. Hard to swallow.

Hard Thing Number One

"What makes a man unclean?" says Jesus to the crowd. "It's not what he puts into his mouth. It's what comes out!"

The Pharisees are offended by this. They consider themselves to be the experts on what makes a man unclean and have quite a long list of what one should and shouldn't put in one's mouth.

Then Jesus' disciples come to him and ask him if he knows that he's upset the Pharisees.

And Jesus says:

Hard Thing Number Two

"If my Father hasn't planted a plant – it will be torn out, roots and all. So leave them. They are blind guides. And you know what? If one blind man leads another, they are both likely to fall into a pit."

This clears up one of the disciples' questions (Do you know you have upset the Pharisees? Yes. Couldn't give a monkey's, actually.)

But Peter has another question: "Could you possibly, maybe, sort of explain the parable to us? You know – the business about what comes out of the mouth?"

And, I promise you, Jesus rolls his eyes here. Or maybe he sighs. Or perhaps he shakes his head. Or quite possibly does a combination of all the above. It's not in the text, but the subtext and the context just scream it out. Particularly when Jesus says:

Hard Thing Number Three

"Are you really that thick?" Jesus asks them. "You put something IN your mouth, you chew it, you swallow it, it goes into your stomach and then it finds its way back out again!

"But what comes OUT of your mouth has its origins in your heart. That's what makes a man unclean.

"And what comes out of the heart? Evil thoughts. Murder. Adultery. Sexual immorality. Theft. Lies. Slander.

"These are the things that make a man unclean, not eating with unwashed hands."

After that, Jesus goes to the region of Tyre and Sidon – Gentile territory. And while he's there, a local woman, a Canaanite, comes to him in great distress.

"Lord!" she cries. "Son of David. Have mercy on me. My daughter is possessed by a demon. She suffers terribly."

Jesus says nothing. Nothing at all. But his disciples are desperate for him to send her away. And they say so.

So Jesus replies with:

Hard Thing Number Four

"The lost sheep of Israel. Those are the only ones I was sent to."

But the woman persists. She kneels before him and cries, "Please, Lord! Help me!"

And Jesus responds by saying:

Hard Thing Number Five

Perhaps the hardest thing of all.

"If you have bread for your children," he says. "It's not right to take it and toss it to the dogs."

And the woman's reply is a blinder.

"Yes Lord," she says. "But surely even dogs get to snack on the crumbs that fall from their master's table."

And Jesus grins, I promise you. And he nods. And there is a twinkle in his eye. It's not in the text, but the subtext and the context shout it like a song of praise.

And then Jesus says:

Hard Thing Number Six

Well, I suppose that the Pharisees would have found it hard, and that the disciples would have done some headscratching, too.

"Woman," he says. "You have great faith. What you ask for is done."

And from that hour, her daughter is healed.

PROPER 16

First reading (Continuous)

Exodus 1:8–2:10

Reader 1: The story begins with a new king *(hum first six notes of "God Save the Queen")*.

Congregation: A new king *(repeat humming)*.

Reader 2: A new king who doesn't know anything about Joseph ascends to the throne of Egypt. And everywhere he looks he sees… Hebrews, God's people.

"Hebrews here. Hebrews there. Hebrews everywhere!" he complains to his people. "You can't throw a rock without hitting a Hebrew. And I don't think that's a very clever state of affairs. If we're not careful, there will soon be more of them than us. And if, by some chance, there is a war, they could join with our enemies and defeat us. No, something must be done about these Hebrews."

Reader 1: So then there are slaves *(hold arms crossed as if bound)*.

Congregation: Slaves *(repeats action)*.

Reader 2: The Hebrews are turned into slaves, put under the control of slave masters, and forced to build great store cities: Pithom and Rameses.

But this does nothing to curb their numbers. In fact, the harder they labour – the more they are oppressed, the more bitterly they are treated – the more the Hebrews multiply. And so the Egyptians fear them even more, and work them ruthlessly – in bricks and mortar and in the fields.

Reader 1: Which brings us to the midwives *(hand to side of mouth, "Call the Midwives!")*.

Congregation: "Call the Midwives!" [And when people are no longer familiar with the television show, you might want to do some fast breathing as if in labour.]

Reader 2: The king sends for the midwives – Shiphrah and Puah were their names. He has a plan, and an awful job for them to do.

"When you deliver the Hebrew children," he said. "Kill the boys, but let the girls live."

But the midwives don't do what the king commands. They fear God and so they let the boys live.

So the king summons them again. "What are you doing?" he shouts. "Why are you letting the boys live?"

"Ah," say the midwives – a clever couple of women, to be sure. "Your Egyptian woman, she waits for the midwife to get there. But these Hebrew women – they're tough. They get on with the births themselves, and the baby arrives before we do!"

God likes that answer – he really does. So he gives the midwives children of their own. And the Hebrews continued to multiply.

Reader 1: And so we come to the River Nile *(make a watery, flowing motion – quite vigorously – with one hand).*

Congregation: The Nile *(repeats motion).*

Reader 2: Pharaoh gives all his people an order. "If a Hebrew gives birth to a boy, throw that baby in the Nile. But let the girls live."

Reader 1: And so a Hebrew couple – a man and a woman from the tribe of Levi – give birth to a baby boy *(waaa!).*

Congregation: A baby boy *(repeats cry).*

Reader 2: For three months, they hide him. And when that is no longer possible, the mother makes a basket out of papyrus. She coats it with tar and pitch to make it waterproof. Then she sets it floating among the reeds along the bank of the Nile. And she asks her daughter to wait, and watch over it.

Reader 1: Then along comes a princess *(OOOOOH!).*

Congregation: A princess *(OOOOOOH!).*

Reader 2: It's Pharaoh's own daughter, about to take a bath in the river. And all her attendants, too.

She sees the basket.

She sends a servant to fetch it.

And when she looks inside, there is a baby boy!

She can tell he's a Hebrew. She knows what she's supposed to do. But when the baby begins to cry, she feels sorry for him.

Reader 1: And that's when the girl who's been watching over the baby pops back into the scene *(Ta–da!)*

Congregation: *Ta–da!*

Reader 2: "I know a Hebrew woman who can nurse him for you," she says.

Pharaoh's daughter agrees. And the girl runs off to find the baby's own mum!

And so she nurses her child, and when he is older, she takes him and gives him to Pharaoh's daughter to be *her* son.

And that's when Pharaoh's daughter gives him his name.

"Moses." That's what she calls him, because she drew him up from the water.

Gospel
....

Matthew 16:13–20

This uses two readers again – one to read the introductory phrase, the other to tell the story.

Reader 1: Jesus had a question:

Reader 2: He and his disciples were in the region of Caesarea Philippi, and he asked them, "The Son of Man – who do people say he is?"

Reader 1: The disciples had an answer – well, three or four answers, actually.

Reader 2: "Some people say John the Baptist," said one of the disciples.

"Some say Elijah," said another.

"I think I recall someone saying Jeremiah," suggested a third.

"One of the prophets, at least," chimed in the others.

Reader 1: Then Jesus had another question:

Reader 2: "But who do you say that I am?"

Reader 1: And Simon Peter answered:

Reader 2: "You? You are the Christ, the Son of the living God."

Reader 1: Then Jesus shared a blessing:

Reader 2: "Simon Bar Jonah," he said. "You are blessed. You didn't come to that conclusion with the help of any man. No, it was my Father who revealed it to you.

"And so I say that you are Peter. I will build my church on this rock. And my church shall not be overcome – not even by the gates of Hades.

"And to you – to you I will give the keys of the kingdom of heaven. What you bind on earth – that will be bound in heaven. What you loose on earth – that will be loosed in heaven, too!"

Reader 1: Then Jesus finished with a warning:

Reader 2: "Tell no one that I am the Christ."

PROPER 17

Psalm (Continuous)

Psalm 105:1–6, 23–26, 45b

This is a psalm we read a few weeks ago (see Proper 14), when the historical reference – the evidence of the thing that God "has done" was to Joseph. This week, the same format is used, except the reference is to another set of verses that use the exodus as an example of what God does.

What I like about this psalm is its emphasis on what God has done – and its quick and powerful retelling of the exodus story (among others) as an example of his mighty deeds. So the reading is designed to emphasize God's mighty acts.

Reader 1: Reads verse 1.

Congregation: Repeats the words "what he has done".

Reader 2: Reads verse 2.

Congregation: Repeats the words "his wonderful acts".

Reader 1: Reads verse 3.

Reader 2: Reads verse 4.

Reader 1: Read verse 5a.

Congregation: Repeats the words "he has done".

Reader 2: Reads verses 5a–6.

Readers 1 and 2: "And this is what he has done."

Reader 1: Reads verse 23.

Reader 2: Reads verse 24.

Reader 1: Reads verse 25.

Reader 2: Reads verse 26.

Reader 1 and 2: "Praise the Lord."

Congregation: Repeats the words "Praise the Lord."

Second reading

....

Romans 12:9–21

The lists that Paul writes can sometimes seem hard to follow. If you're sitting listening to them they just seem to run into each other. So this reading is designed to help the congregation pay a little more attention to each item individually.

I think it would be fun to have one person to read each command, and another person to "embody" it in some way. It would work really well if the reader is a kind of "straight man" and the other person mostly does the funny stuff.

Reader: Love must be sincere.
(Other person puts arm around him and says, as sincerely as he can, "I love you man. I really do. No I mean it. Really.")

Reader: Hate what is evil;
(Reader holds up sign that says "Evil". Other person says, "Oooh, ick, yuck – can't stand that evil stuff." Then he grabs sign and throws it to the ground.)

Reader: Cling to what is good.
(Reader holds up another sign that says "Good". Other person grabs it and hugs it and won't let go, and says, "I'm clinging to what is good!")

Reader: Be devoted to one another in love.
(Other person puts arm around him again and says, "I'm devoted to you man, I really am. No I mean it. Really.")

Reader: Honour one another above yourselves.
(Other person says to reader, "You're amazing, man. On a pedestal. I mean it. Really.")

Reader: Never be lacking in zeal,
(Other person shouts, "Yeah!")

Reader: But keep your spiritual fervour,
("Yeah! Yeah!")

Reader: Serving the Lord.
(Other person goes to say "Yeah!" again, and gets a "look" from reader. Then says, "Oh, I see, it's actually about DOING something. Yeah.")

Reader: Be joyful in hope,
(Other person, big smile, says, "I'm joyful! I hope.")

Reader: Patient in affliction,
(Other person says, "Owww. It's okay. I'm dealing with it man.")

Reader: Faithful in prayer.
(Other person holds hands in praying position. Bows head. Shuts eyes. Reader pauses. Other person peeps and says, "How long do you want me to do this? Oh, I see… faithful. Right." Shuts eyes again. Reader eventually moves on. After much peeping and waiting reader continues.)

Reader: Share with the Lord's people who are in need.
(Other person runs puts arm around reader and tucks a paper note into his top pocket. Says, "I can tell you need this man. I really can. It's my pleasure. Really." Leaves arm there.)

Reader: Practise hospitality.
(Other person says, "And you can come over for pizza anytime you like.")

Reader: Bless those who persecute you;
(Reader punches other person on the arm. Other person shouts, "Hey! Why'd you do that, you rotten… flippin' –")

Reader *(interrupting)***:** Bless and do not curse.
(Other person claps hand over his mouth and mutters, "Oh, I see.")

Reader: Rejoice with those who rejoice;
(Reader goes "Hooray'" and nudges other person who then joins in "Hooray!")

Reader: Mourn with those who mourn.
(Reader rubs corner of eye, and pretends to cry; nudges other person who joins in.)

Reader: Live in harmony with one another.
(If possible, they sing two notes in harmony – even if they're off, it will still be funny!)

Reader: Do not be proud, but be willing to associate with people of low position.
(Other person puts arm around reader. Says "It's okay man, I'm still happy to associate with you. I really am.")

Reader *(giving other person that sarcastic "look" again)***:** Do not be conceited.
(Other person removes arm, says, "Ah yes, I see.")

Reader: Do not repay anyone evil for evil.
(Punches other person on arm again, who goes to return punch and then says, "Nope, not getting me this time!")

Reader: Be careful to do what is right in the eyes of everyone.
(Other person looks at crowd, points and says "Everyone? Even that guy?")

Reader: If it is possible, as far as it depends on you, live at peace with everyone.
(Other person looks at reader, gives him peace sign and says "Peace, Dude.")

Reader: Do not take revenge, my dear friends,
(Punches other person again, who says "I have so got this one, man. I am chilled.")

Reader: But leave room for God's wrath, for it is written: "It is mine to avenge; I will repay," says the Lord.
(Other person looks up to the sky and says, "It's all down to you, Lord." Then takes a step away from reader.)

Reader: On the contrary: "If your enemy is hungry, feed him;
(Other person forces some small biscuit or something into mouth of reader, or maybe a stick of gum.)

Reader: "If he is thirsty, give him something to drink.
(Other person sticks one of those water bottles with a pull-up top into reader's mouth and gives him a squirt.)

Reader: "In doing this, you will heap burning coals on his head."
(Other person looks around and then shrugs.)

Reader: Do not be overcome by evil,
(Punches other person one last time.)

Reader: But overcome evil with good.
(Other person puts arm around reader one last time and says, "I love you man, I really do. I mean it. Really".)

PROPER 18

Psalm (Related)

Psalm 119: 33–40

For this psalm you will need a reader who reads the first part of each verse and demonstrates the action that goes with it. The congregation then repeats those words and the action, and the reader reads the rest of the verse.

Reader: "Teach me" *(then reaches out hands and pulls them back towards chest as if receiving something).*

Congregation: "Teach me" *(repeats the action).*

Reader: "Teach me, O Lord, the way of your decrees
that I may follow it to the end."

Reader: "Give me understanding" *(and points finger to head).*

Congregation: "Give me understanding" *(repeats the action).*

Reader: "Give me understanding, so that I may keep your law
and obey it with all my heart."

Reader: "Direct me" *(point in some direction, as if showing the way).*

Congregation: "Direct me" *(repeats the action).*

Reader: "Direct me in the path of your commands,
for there I find delight."

Reader: "Turn my heart" *(puts hand on heart and turns body).*

Congregation: "Turn my heart" *(repeats the action).*

Reader: "Turn my heart toward your statutes
and not toward selfish gain."

Reader: "Turn my eyes" *(holds head with both hands and turns).*

Congregation: "Turn my eyes" *(repeats the action).*

Reader: "Turn my eyes away from worthless things;
preserve my life according to your word."

Reader: "Fulfil your promise" *(raises hand in air and then clenches fist).*

Congregation: "Fulfil your promise" *(repeats the action).*

Reader: "Fulfil your promise to your servant,
so that you may be feared."

Reader: "Take away" *(pretends to grab hold of something and cast it away).*

Congregation: "Take away" *(repeats the action).*

Reader: "Take away the disgrace I dread,
for your laws are good."

Reader: "How I long" *(reaches both hands out in imploring fashion).*

Congregation: "How I long" *(repeats the action).*

Reader: "How I long for your precepts!
In your righteousness preserve my life."

Gospel
....

Matthew 18:15–20

Reader: Here's what Jesus said:
   "If your brother sins against you, go to him, tell him what he's done. Sort it out, just the two of you."

Congregation: That's fine, if he'll talk to me.

Reader: Exactly. If you sort it out, you can be brothers again.

Congregation: Yeah, but what if he won't listen to me?

Reader: If he won't listen, take two or three others with you. That way, there will be witnesses to your conversation. It won't be one of those "he said, she said" things.

Congregation: And if that doesn't work?

Reader: Take the matter to the whole church.

Congregation: And what if…?

Reader: If that doesn't work, if he refuses to even discuss it and try to work it out, there's not much more you can do but treat him like a pagan or a tax collector.

Congregation: All right then.

Reader: This is the truth. What you bind on earth gets bound in heaven. What you loose on earth gets loosed in heaven.

Congregation: Really? That's amazing!

Reader: Really. If two of you agree on anything, my Father in heaven will do it. It only takes a few – two or three of you – together in my name. And I'm there with you!

PROPER 19

First reading (Continuous)

Exodus 14:19–31

You need two readers here. Use the alternating voices to show the ebb and flow of the action.

Reader 1: It's like a game of chess, or Risk, or Battleship, although it's deadly serious and not a game at all. Everyone moves into position. We know how it ends, but for those who are there, standing at the edge of the sea, the outcome is far from certain.

Reader 2: The angel of God makes the first move. He's been travelling in front of Israel's army. But now he moves to the rear. As does the pillar of cloud, so that it stands between the armies of Egypt and Israel – bringing darkness to the former and light to the latter – and so keeping them apart.

Reader 1: Moses makes the next move. He stretches his hand over the sea. And in response, God sets the east wind blowing, all through the night. The wind divides the water, clears a dry path down the middle.

Reader 2: And the Israelites walk down that path, on dry ground, with a wall of water on the right and a wall of water on the left.

Reader 1: Then the Egyptians make their countermove. They follow the Israelites down the dry path – their horses, their chariots, their horsemen.

Reader 2: But God is ready for them. Looking down from the pillar of cloud and fire, he throws them into confusion. He tears off their chariot wheels.

Reader 1: And, in a panic, the Egyptians decide to flee. "Let's leave the Israelites!" they cry. "The Lord is fighting for them."

Reader 2: But it's too late. The Lord tells Moses to stretch out his hand again. And when, at daybreak, he does, the waters flow back into place; they flow over the horses and the chariots and the horsemen – the whole of Pharaoh's army that had followed Israel into the sea. And not one of them survives.

Reader 1: So the Israelites walk through the sea – walls of water on their left and right. And with that same sea, the Lord slays the Egyptians, and leaves their corpses on the shore.

Reader 2: And when the Israelites see this – God's great power displayed against the Egyptians – they trust him, and Moses his servant.

Psalm (Related)

Psalm 103:[1–7] 8–13

Again, this lends itself to using two readers: one to make the general statement about the Lord's character, the other to list the specific examples. If you want them to be more involved, the congregation could join in with either reader throughout, or with just the last verse.

Reader 1: Reads verses 1–2.

Reader 2: Reads verses 3–5.

Reader 1: Reads verse 6.

Reader 2: Reads verse 7.

Reader 1: Reads verses 8–9.

Reader 2: Reads verses 10–12.

Both (or all): Read verse 13.

PROPER 20

First reading (Related)

Jonah 3:10–4:11

Reader 1: It sounds like a happy ending.

Reader 2: The people of Nineveh turn from their evil ways. God sees it. His anger turns to compassion. And he chooses not to destroy them.

Reader 1: It sounds like a happy ending. But Jonah isn't happy.

Reader 2: In fact he's downright angry. "I knew this would happen!" he prays (although it sounds a bit more like a rant). "That's why I ran away to Tarshish in the first place! You're gracious, God, and compassionate and loving and slow to anger and desperate not to destroy."
    And then he adds, "So kill me now, Lord. I'm better off dead than alive."
    And God replies, "Sorry, but do you really have any right to be angry?"

Reader 1: It sounds like a happy ending. But Jonah isn't happy. Not happy at all. So he stamps off in a huff.

Reader 2: He finds a place, east of Nineveh. A place where he can wait and watch and see. He builds himself a little shelter – he's committed to being there until his not-so-friendly hopes for the city are realized.
    And God humours him. He grows a little vine over Jonah. And Jonah is pleased.

Reader 1: It sounds like a happy ending again.

Reader 2: But then God sends a worm to chew on the vine. And when the vine has withered and died, and Jonah no longer enjoys its shade, God sends a blazing hot sun and a scorching east wind, and Jonah grows faint in the heat.
    "Kill me now!" he cries again. "I'm better off dead than alive."

Reader 1: It sounded like a happy ending. And you have to wonder if God considered doing this, for even a second – just to be free of the man's incessant moaning.

Reader 2: But he doesn't kill Jonah. No, he asks him that question again.

"Do you really have any right to be angry?"

And Jonah is sure that he does. "Angry enough to die," he insists (which is pretty angry).

So God, more or less, asks "Why?"

"You are concerned about this vine," he says. "Even though you had nothing to do with it growing. You didn't tend it or water it. It sprang up overnight. And, overnight, it died.

"But there are over a hundred and twenty thousand people in Nineveh, Jonah. And their cattle. A hundred and twenty thousand people who don't know their right hand from their left. Should not I be concerned about them?"

Reader 1: And then the story ends. Happily ever after, or not? The choice is up to Jonah, I guess. And maybe up to you and me, as well.

Are we concerned about our own comfort. And our own prejudices?

Or are we concerned for God's concerns?

Gospel
....

Matthew 20:1–16

You will need three readers and lots of hats! The first reader will be both the narrator and the owner of the vineyard. The second reader represents the men who were hired first. And the third reader (the one with all the hats) will be the men who were hired later.

Reader 1: "This is what the kingdom of heaven is like," said Jesus. "It's like a man who owned a field and went out, early one morning, to hire workers. He found some men, and agreed to pay them a denarius for a day's work."

Reader 2: "Pleasure doing business with you." *(Shakes hand of owner. Then he turns away and pretends to dig, wiping forehead and occasionally saying, "It's hot!" This continues through rest of "hiring".)*

Reader 1: About the third hour, he found some more men, standing around in the marketplace. They weren't doing anything and, when he asked them why, they explained.

Reader 3: "Nobody's hired us."

Reader 1: So he asked them to work for him, too. And agreed to pay them, as well.

Reader 3: "Thanks, boss." *(Shakes hand.)*

Reader 1: He found some more men at the sixth hour…

Reader 3 *(with different hat)***:** "We won't let you down." *(Shakes hand.)*

Reader 1: And at the ninth hour…

Reader 3 *(with yet another hat)***:** "Ta, very much, guv." *(Shakes hand.)*

Reader 1: And he hired them, as well. Then, at the eleventh hour, he found even more men just standing around. "Why aren't you doing anything?" he asked them.

Reader 3 *(different hat)***:** "Because no one has hired us."

Reader 1: So he hired them, too.

Reader 3: "We'll do our best." *(Shakes hand.)*

Reader 1: When evening came, the man told his foreman to call in all the workers and pay them, starting with the last who'd been hired. The workers hired at the eleventh hour were each given a denarius.

Reader 3: "Cheers. Thanks. You can call on us any time!"

Reader 1: When they saw this, the men who were hired first were delighted.

Reader 2 *(who has stopped working – rubs hands together)***:** "This is looking good! If he got a denarius for working just an hour, imagine how much we'll get!" *(tries to calculate – counting on fingers, or a pretend calculator)*.

Reader 1: But each of them received only the one denarius they were promised. And they were not happy. Not one little bit.

Reader 2: "Now hang on. They only worked for an hour and they got the same money as those of us who worked the whole day. In the sun. The really hot sun. That was hot. And sweaty. And hot."

Reader 1: But the man answered. "You might think I'm being unfair, but I'm not. You agreed to work the whole day for a denarius. That's what you got. So take it and go. If I want to give the same to the last man I hired, that's my right. It's my money after all. It's not my problem if you have a problem with my generosity."

"And so," said Jesus, "the last will be first. And the first will be last."

(Readers 2 and 3 swap places, perhaps with Reader 2 still grumbling, "It's not fair. It was really hot. Look, I have a blister…")

PROPER 21

Psalm (Continuous)

Psalm 78:1–4, 12–16

You will need two readers. One to read the passage and the other to echo him, do the actions, and then lead the congregation in repeating the actions. It will help if the second reader familiarizes himself with the actions so that he speaks and acts simultaneously. Begin by telling the congregation to watch the second reader as they will have to repeat his words and actions. I suggest you practise with the first verse.

Verse 1

Reader 1: O my people, hear my teaching;
listen to the words of my mouth.

Reader 2: My mouth *(pointing finger at mouth)*.

Congregation: *(Repeats words and actions.)*

Verse 2

Reader 1: I will open my mouth…

Reader 2: My mouth *(pointing finger at mouth)*.

Congregation: *(Repeats words and actions.)*

Reader 1: I will utter hidden things…

Reader 2: Things from of old – *(turning away and concealing something against chest)*.

Congregation: *(Repeats words and actions.)*

Verse 3

Reader 1: Things we have heard and known,

Reader 2: Things we have heard *(point at ear)* and known *(point to side of head).*

Congregation: *(Repeats words and actions.)*

Reader 1: Things our fathers have told us.

Verse 4

Reader 1: We will not hide them from their children;

Reader 2: We will not hide *(repeat hiding action and then fling hands open to reveal what is hidden).*

Congregation: *(Repeats words and actions.)*

Reader 1: We will tell the next generation
the praiseworthy deeds of the Lord,

Reader 2: The praiseworthy deeds! *(shouting and throwing hands in air in praise).*

Congregation: *(Repeats words and actions.)*

Reader 1: His power, and the wonders he has done.

Verse 12 (yes, we're jumping a few verses!)

Reader 1: He did miracles in the sight of their fathers

Reader 2: In the sight of their fathers *(pointing to eyes).*

Congregation: *(Repeats words and actions.)*

Reader 1: In the land of Egypt, in the region of Zoan.

Verse 13

Reader 1: He divided the sea and led them through;

Reader 2: He divided the sea *(bringing down hand as if in karate chop).*

Congregation: *(Repeats words and actions.)*

Reader 1: He made the water stand firm like a wall.

Reader 2: Like a wall *(hold hands with palms out, as if miming a wall).*

Congregation: *(Repeats words and actions.)*

Verse 14

Reader 1: He guided them with the cloud by day

Reader 2: With the cloud *(make cloud shape with hands/finger).*

Congregation: *(Repeats words and actions.)*

Reader 1: And with light from the fire all night.

Reader 2: Light from the fire *(suggest flickering flames with fingers).*

Congregation: *(Repeats words and actions.)*

Verse 15

Reader 1: He split the rocks in the desert
and gave them water as abundant as the seas;

Reader 2: Abundant as the seas *(make wave motion with hands).*

Congregation: *(Repeats words and actions.)*

Verse 16

Reader 1: He brought streams out of a rocky crag
and made water flow down like rivers.

Reader 2: Like rivers *(throwing out arms like rushing waters).*

Congregation: *(Repeats words and actions.)*

Gospel
....

Matthew 21:23–32

You will need four readers for this one. A narrator, Jesus, one to represent the chief priests, and another for the elders.

Narrator: Jesus went into the temple courts. He began to teach. And while he was doing so, the chief priests and the elders approached him with a question.

Chief Priests: "What is your authority for doing the things you do?"

Elders: "And who gave you that authority?"

Jesus: "I'll tell you what, I've got a question for you. You answer my question, and I'll be happy to answer yours. Here it is: 'Was John's baptism something sent from heaven. Or was it just one man's idea?'"

Chief Priests: "Oh, dear. If we say it came from heaven, then he will surely ask why we didn't believe in it."

Elders: "And if we say it was just a man's idea, then the people will turn on us – for they think John was a prophet, sent by God."

Narrator: So they turned to Jesus, shrugged their shoulders and said:

Chief Priests and Elders: "Dunno."

Narrator: So Jesus replied:

Jesus: "Fine. Then I won't answer your question, either. But I will tell you a story.
     "Once there was a man with two sons.
     "'I want you to go and work in my vineyard,' he said to the first son.
     "And the first son said, 'No!' But, later, he changed his mind and went anyway.
     "The man said the same thing to his second son.
     "'I will do what you ask.' the son agreed. But later, he changed his mind and did not go.
     "Now which of the two sons did what his father wanted him to do?"

Chief Priests and Elders: "The first son."

Jesus: "And so, like that first son, the tax collectors and prostitutes at first refused God's way. But when John came, preaching righteousness and repentance, they believed and changed.

"But you, like the second son, agreed to God's ways. Then, when John came, you refused to believe, refused to change, even when you saw the difference in their lives.

"And that's why I say that tax collectors and prostitutes will go into the kingdom of God before you."

PROPER 22

First reading (Continuous)

Exodus 20:1–4, 7–9, 12–20

It starts with God. It always does. And so God speaks:

"I'm the one who brought you out of Egypt," he says. "You were slaves. And I, the Lord your God, am the one who set you free. So this is how you should treat me:

"You should worship me alone, and no other god before me.

"Don't make any idols, either – fashioned in the form of some thing from heaven or the earth or sea.

"Treat my name carefully. For if you misuse it, you will have me to reckon with.

"And remember – the Sabbath day is holy. You have six days to do your work. Keep the seventh special, set apart."

"Now here's how you should treat each other:

"Give special honour to your parents – your mother and your father. Do that and you will prosper in the land I give you.

"Do not murder.

"Do not be unfaithful to your spouse.

"Do not take what isn't yours.

"Do not lie about your neighbour.

"Be grateful for what you have – set aside your desire for what belongs to your neighbour – his wife, his manservant, his maidservant, his ox, his donkey – in fact, anything he owns."

It starts with God. And in response to his presence – to the thunder and the lightning and the sound of the trumpets and the smoke – the people tremble with fear.

They keep their distance. "Speak to us, yourself," they say to Moses. "And we will listen. But don't let God speak to us. For if he does, we will die."

"Don't be afraid," Moses replies. "God has simply come to test you – for he knows that if you understand who he is, if you fear him – then that will keep you from sinning."

Psalm (Continuous)

Psalm 19

You will need two readers for this psalm. In the first part of the psalm, the first reader essentially states the case – establishes the principle – that God is revealed through his *creation*. And then the second reader describes a specific example of that principle, which the psalmist has chosen.

Starting at verse 7, the same pattern is used, as the first reader describes God's revelation through his *law* and the second reader shows a specific example.

Reader 1: Reads verses 1–4a.

Reader 2: Reads verses 4b–6. *(It might help for the reader to use a few actions here: to point to the rising sun, maybe even to make the shape of a tent with her fingers, to wave to the bridegroom as he leaves the tent, and then to trace the course of the champion racing across the sky – pointing with a finger from one side to the other.)*

Reader 1: Reads verse 7a: "The law of the Lord is perfect,"

Reader 2: Reads the rest of verse 7a: "Refreshing the soul" *(lift two hands up from chest into the air).*

Reader 1: Reads verse 7b: "The statutes of the Lord are trustworthy,"

Reader 2: Reads the rest of verse 7b: "Making wise the simple" *(point to head).*

Reader 1: Reads verse 8a: "The precepts of the Lord are right,"

Reader 2: Reads the rest of verse 8a: "Giving joy to the heart" *(put hand on heart and smile).*

Reader 1: Reads verse 8b: "The commands of the Lord are radiant,"

Reader 2: Reads the rest of verse 8b: "Giving light to the eyes" *(point to eyes).*

Reader 1: Reads verse 9a: "The fear of the Lord is pure,"

Reader 2: Reads the rest of verse 9a: "Enduring forever" *(stretch arm out in front of you).*

Reader 1: Reads verse 9b, just "The decrees of the Lord are firm,"

Reader 2: Reads the rest of verse 9b:"And all of them are righteous" *(hold finger in air).*

Reader 1: Reads verse 10.

Reader 2: Reads verse 11.

Reader 1: Reads verses 12–13a.

Reader 2: Reads verse 13b.

Both: Read verse 14.

Alternative version

This approach uses only one reader and builds a lovely time of worship into the reading.

Reader: Reads verses 1–6. Then everyone sings a few songs about creation.

Reader: Reads verses 7–11. Then everyone sings a few songs about the life God calls us to live or songs that reflect on his law and wisdom.

Reader: Reads verse 12–13. This is followed by a time of prayerful confession, ending with a song related to confession and forgiveness.

Then the whole congregation joins the reader in verse 14.

PROPER 23

First Reading (Continuous)

Exodus 32:1–14

The story begins. The people are curious.

"What's keeping Moses?" they ask his brother Aaron. "He's been up that mountain a very long time. He brought us out of Egypt, yes – but now what's happened to him?"

And so they make a request – a request that's rather spurious.

"Seeing as Moses seems to have disappeared, why don't we make ourselves some gods to lead us?"

So Aaron puts out a call for earrings – loads and loads of earrings. Gold earrings from wives and sons and daughters. Every earring they can find. Then he melts them down and casts them into the shape of a calf. And he announces that this is the god whose power brought them out of Egypt.

And then, to make things worse, he builds an altar in front of the calf. And the next day, everyone brings offerings to the calf-god and burns sacrifices to him. And then they have a party.

This does not impress the true God of Israel one little bit. In fact, it makes him furious.

He tells Moses what the people are up to – how they have been corrupted and have disobeyed his commands. How they have made an idol and offered sacrifices to it and given it credit for delivering them from the Egyptians.

At which point, he threatens to do something quite injurious.

"Stiff–necked, that's what these people are!" God says. "So I think you should leave me for a bit, Moses. Let my anger simmer and sizzle and burn. Then I will destroy them and make you into a great nation, instead."

Which prompts a question from Moses – a question that arises because he is... well... curious.

"Why let your anger burn against your people when you went to all that trouble to deliver them from Egypt? And speaking of Egypt, what will the Egyptians think when they hear that you freed your people only to destroy them in the desert?

"Please reconsider. Please don't destroy them. And remember your promise – to Abraham, Isaac and Jacob – that you would make a great nation, not from me, but from them."

So God relented and did not destroy his people.

First reading (Related)

Isaiah 25:1–9

Reader 1: Reads verse 1.

Reader 2: Reads verse 2.

Reader 1: Reads verse 3.

Reader 2: Reads verses 4–5.

Reader 1: Reads verse 6.

Reader 2: Reads verse 7–8a, ending at "he will swallow up death forever".

Reader 1: Reads rest of verse 8.

Both: Read verse 9.

PROPER 24

First reading (Continuous)

Exodus 33:12–23

This is a conversation, so you will need two readers. The first one reads what Moses says (more-or-less) and the second reads what God says. The key is to make it sound like a conversation not a Bible reading!

Reader 1: Reads verses 12–13.

Reader 2: Reads verse 14.

Reader 1: Reads verses 15–16.

Reader 2: Reads 17.

Reader 1: Reads verse 18.

Reader 2: Reads verses 19–23.

Gospel

Matthew 22:15–22

Divide the congregation into two groups. One is the Road Runner, famous from children's cartoons, and the other is his arch-enemy, Wile E. Coyote. The first group says "Beep-beep" when the reader mentions the Road Runner; the other holds up a pretend sign and says "Yikes" when he mentions coyote. A helper is needed to lead each group in at the right time.

It's a bit like one of those Road Runner cartoons *("Beep-beep")*.
    Jesus is the Road Runner *("Beep–beep")*.
    And the Pharisees are Wile E. Coyote *(hold up pretend sign and say "Yikes!")*.

And so, much like Wile E. Coyote *("Yikes!")*, the Pharisees try to devise a trap for Jesus. They send some of their followers and also a group of Herodians to ask him a question.

And the question is about as long and convoluted as one of those Acme devices favoured by the coyote *("Yikes!")*.

"Teacher," they say. "You are a man of integrity. You teach the way of God. You teach the truth. You aren't worried about what people think of you. Their position and rank mean nothing to you. So give us your opinion, please, on this very important matter: Is it right for us to pay taxes to Caesar?"

The trap is set. Jesus stands the chance, on the one hand, of alienating the people, oppressed by their Roman rulers. And on the other hand, he stands the chance of being accused of sedition, of stirring up a rebellion.

But he is the Road Runner, remember? *("Beep-beep")*.

And he instantly recognizes the trap that this pack of coyotes *("Yikes!")* has set for him.

And so he calls their bluff.

"You hypocrites! This is not an honest question – it is nothing but an attempt to trap me."

Then he turns the trap on them.

"Bring me a coin," he says. And when one of them finally fishes a denarius out of his money bag and hands it over, Jesus asks a question of his own.

"Whose face is on this coin? And whose name?"

"Caesar's," they answer.

"Then give to Caesar what belongs to Caesar. And to God what belongs to God."

So the trap fails. The coyotes are gutted *("Yikes")*.

And, once again, the Road Runner gets away *("Beep-beep")*.

PROPER 25

First reading (Related)

Leviticus 19:1–2, 15–18

God said to Moses, "Here is what I want you to tell the people of Israel: I, the Lord your God, am holy, and because of that, I want you to be holy, too.

"Do not pervert justice. Don't show favouritism either to the rich or the poor. Be fair when you judge your neighbour.

"Don't go about slandering people.

"Don't do anything that puts your neighbour's life at risk. I am the Lord.

"Don't hold hate for your brother in your heart. And if your neighbour does something wrong, tell him off plainly. That way you won't share in his guilt.

"And don't hold a grudge or seek revenge against one of your people. Instead, love your neighbour as you love yourself. I am the Lord."

Gospel

Matthew 22:34–46

This reading picks up, more-or-less, from last week's reading, and I thought it would be fun to keep the Road Runner theme going. So, once again, divide the congregation into two groups – one is the Road Runner, who says "Beep-beep" when the Road Runner is mentioned, and the other group is Wile E. Coyote, who holds up a pretend sign and says "Yikes" whenever coyote is mentioned. As before, a helper is needed to lead each group in at the right time.

It's a bit like one of those Road Runner cartoons *("Beep–beep")*.

Jesus is the Road Runner *("Beep–beep")*.

And the Pharisees are Wile E. Coyote *(hold up pretend sign and say "Yikes!")*.

When the Pharisees, those Wile E. Coyotes *("Yikes!"),* discover that Jesus the Road Runner *("Beep–beep")* has escaped the trap the Sadducees laid for him, they go to Acme and come up with another trap.

An expert in the law, a particularly clever coyote *(Yikes!)* asks Jesus a question: "Which is the greatest commandment in the law?"

Jesus the Road Runner *("Beep–beep!")* offers a quick reply:

"The first, the greatest commandment? Love the Lord your God. With all your heart. With all your soul. With all your mind.

"And the second is like it. Love your neighbour like you love yourself.

"Everything in the Law and the Prophets hangs, suspended and extended, from these two commands."

Then, much like the Road Runner *("Beep–beep"),* Jesus uses their trap to turn the trap on them.

"While we're all here, I have a question for you," he says. "A question about the Messiah. Whose son do you think he is?"

"The son of David," say the coyotes *("Yikes!"),* falling into the trap.

Jesus grins *("Beep–beep").* "So why then does David, inspired by the Spirit, call the Messiah 'Lord'?"

Then he springs the trap, with the flick of a verse (Psalm 110:1, to be precise).

"The Lord said to my Lord

Sit at my right hand

Until I put your enemies

under your feet."

"If David calls the Messiah 'Lord'," Jesus asks. "Then how can the Messiah be his son?"

And with that little sign in their hands *("Yikes"),* the Pharisees fall off the proverbial cliff, there's a little proverbial thud, and proverbial puff of smoke at the bottom. And they decide to ask him no further questions.

'Cause he's Jesus – the Road Runner *("Beep–beep!").*

LAST SUNDAY AFTER TRINITY IF OBSERVED AS BIBLE SUNDAY

First reading

Nehemiah 8:1–4a [5–6] 8–12

This is another two-hander for Bible Sunday.

Reader 1: The story starts at the Water Gate. Water? Get it? It's what you need to live. As the deer pants for the water…

Reader 2: The gate has been recently reconstructed, along with the rest of Jerusalem's gates and walls. There's a big square in the city, in front of the Water Gate, and all the Israelites gather there – "as one man" (that's what the passage says). And they tell Ezra the priest to bring out the Book of the Law of Moses.

Reader 1: And then there is one incredibly lengthy Bible reading session.

Reader 2: From daybreak till noon – that's how long Ezra reads aloud from the Book of the Law of Moses – on the first day of the seventh month. With men and women and all who could understand gathered in front of him. And the passage says that they listened attentively.

Reader 1: And they didn't just listen – they responded wholeheartedly.

Reader 2: Ezra was standing on a wooden platform, built specially for the occasion – so that everyone could see.
And when he opened the book, everybody stood up.
Ezra praised God, and everybody lifted their hands and shouted "Amen! Amen!"

And then everybody bowed down and worshipped the Lord.

Reader 1: And Ezra wasn't the only one who read from the book.

Reader 2: The Levites read from it, too – and explained it, so that everyone could understand what it meant.

Reader 1: And when they heard the word of God and understood it, the people began to weep.

Reader 2: But the governor, Nehemiah, along with Ezra the priest and the Levites told them to stop weeping.

Reader 1: In fact, they told the people to party, instead!

Reader 2: "This day is sacred to the Lord," said Nehemiah. "And the JOY of the Lord is our strength! So eat and drink and send food to those who haven't prepared any."

Reader 1: So that's what the people did. They ate the best food and drank the sweetest drinks and sent food to others and celebrated. All because they understood the word of the Lord.

Reader 2: And I don't know about you, but I wouldn't mind being a part of a worship service like that one!

Psalm
....

Psalm 119:1–16

You will need two readers for this one – and lots of Bibles! Ideally, everyone in the church should have a Bible in their hands. If you have pew Bibles, that makes things easy. If not, the previous week you might want to ask everyone to bring a Bible along on this Sunday. And, if "push comes to shove", tell everyone who doesn't have a Bible to open their hands as if they are holding a pretend Bible!

The first reader reads the text, and whenever she gets to a part that mentions God's word or law or precepts or statutes, reader two repeats that phrase and holds his open Bible in the air, celebrating it as if it's something special – because it is! And the congregation joins in on that action. You will have to explain this to them, of course, before you begin the reading. And you might even want to practise with one verse, to show them how it works. They don't have to say anything, all they have to do is lift up their open Bibles.

Reader 1: Blessed are those whose ways are blameless,
who walk according to the law of the Lord.

Reader 2 *(holds up Bible and says)***:** His law

Reader 1: Blessed are those who keep his statutes

Reader 2 *(holds up Bible and says)***:** His statutes

Reader 1: And seek him with all their heart –
they do no wrong
but follow his ways.

Reader 2 *(holds up Bible and says)***:** His ways

Reader 1: You have laid down precepts

Reader 2 *(holds up Bible and says)***:** Your precepts

Reader 1: That are to be fully obeyed.
Oh, that my ways were steadfast
in obeying your decrees!

Reader 2 *(holds up Bible and says)***:** Your decrees

Reader 1: Then I would not be put to shame
when I consider all your commands.

Reader 2 *(holds up Bible and says)***:** Your commands

Reader 1: I will praise you with an upright heart
as I learn your righteous laws.

Reader 2 *(holds up Bible and says)***:** Your righteous laws

Reader 1: I will obey your decrees;

Reader 2 *(holds up Bible and says)***:** Your decrees

Reader 1: Do not utterly forsake me.
How can a young person stay on the path of purity?
By living according to your word.

Reader 2 *(holds up Bible and says)***:** Your word

Reader 1: I seek you with all my heart;
do not let me stray from your commands.

Reader 2 *(holds up Bible and says)*: Your commands

Reader 1: I have hidden your word

Reader 2 *(holds up Bible and says)*: Your word

Reader 1: In my heart
that I might not sin against you.
Praise be to you, Lord;
teach me your decrees.

Reader 2 *(holds up Bible and says)*: Your decrees

Reader 1: With my lips I recount
all the laws

Reader 2 *(holds up Bible and says)*: All the laws

Reader 1: That come from your mouth.
    I rejoice in following your statutes

Reader 2 *(holds up Bible and says)*: Your statutes

Reader 1: As one rejoices in great riches.
I meditate on your precepts

Reader 2 *(holds up Bible and says)*: Your precepts

Reader 1: And consider your ways.
    I delight in your decrees;

Reader 2 *(holds up Bible and says)*: Your decrees

Reader 1: I will not neglect your word.

Reader 2 *(holds up Bible and says)*: Your word.

Alternative version

You will need two readers to present this reading which I've adapted for Bible Sunday.

Reader 1: In 1 Timothy 3:16, Paul tells us that the word of God is "useful". Psalm 119 tells us how:
For purity

Reader 2: Reads verse 9.

Reader 1: For living the right way

Reader 2: Reads verse 10.

Reader 1: For holiness

Reader 2: Reads verse 11.

Reader 1: For teaching us who God is, so we know how and why to praise him.

Reader 2: Reads verse 12.

Reader 1: For knowing what to pass on to the next generation.

Reader 2: Reads verse 13.

Reader 1: For finding true wealth

Reader 2: Reads verse 14.

Reader 1: For meditation

Reader 2: Reads verse 15.

Reader 1: For joy and delight.

Reader 2: Reads verse 16.

Reader 1 *(says to congregation)***:** Now let's all say that final verse together.

All: Say verse 16.

ALL SAINTS' DAY

First reading

Revelation 7:9–17

You will need two readers – one to read the narrative parts of the text, and the other to lead the congregation in the spoken parts. It might even be nice to break the congregation up into two groups and have half read the words of the multitude and the other half read the words of the angels. At the end everyone reads the description of the saints.

Reader 1: Reads verses 9–10a.

Reader 2/Group 1: Reads 10b (the bit in quotes).

Reader 1: Reads verse 11 and first word of verse 12.

Reader 2/Group 2: Reads rest of verse 12 (the bit in quotes again).

Reader 1: Reads verses 13 and first part of verse 14 (ending at "Sir, you know").

Reader 2 (and whole congregation): Reads rest of verse 14 to end of verse 17.

Gospel

Matthew 5:1–12

Again, this uses two readers – one to lead half the congregation in their actions for the first part of each Beatitude and the other to lead the rest of the congregation in the actions for the second part. As with other readings of this kind, it always helps to practise one of the verses with the congregation to give them an idea of how everything works.

Reader 1: Now when Jesus saw the crowds, he went up on a mountainside and sat down. His disciples came to him, and he began to teach them, saying:

"Blessed are the poor in spirit,"
(Following this line, hold out hand with sad expression on face and say, "Buddy, can you spare a dime?" or pretend to hold out magazine and say "Big Issue?" Then the congregation do the action, too.)

Reader 2: "For theirs is the kingdom of heaven."
(Point to heaven and shout "Where God gets his way!" Congregation repeats.)

Reader 1: "Blessed are those who mourn,"
(Wipe eyes with fists, sad face. Congregation repeats.)

Reader 2: "For they will be comforted."
(Put arm around Reader 1 and pat on head, say "It will be all right." Congregation repeats.)

Reader 1: "Blessed are the meek,"
(Hold up finger, make tiny little mouse-like voice "I'm meek". Congregation repeats.)

Reader 2: "For they will inherit the earth."
(Pretend to carry earth – arms as if around enormous globe. Go "Whoa!" or "Oh yeah!" Congregation repeats.)

Reader 1: "Blessed are those who hunger and thirst for righteousness,"
(Rub tummy and make tummy-growling sound. Congregation repeats.)

Reader 2: "For they will be filled."
(Make gobbling up or full belly motion. Congregation repeats.)

Reader 1: "Blessed are the merciful,"
(Say to Reader 2 "It's okay, I forgive you." Congregation does the same to Group 2.)

Reader 2: "For they will be shown mercy."
(Return the "It's okay, I forgive you" favour to Reader 1 and Group 1.)

Reader 1: "Blessed are the pure in heart,"
(Act as if pulling your heart from chest (remember "Indiana Jones"? Then hold it up in the air, point to it and say, "100 per cent pure!" Congregation repeats.)

Reader 2: "For they will see God."
(Shade eyes as if looking for something, then say "There he is! Wow. Congregation repeats.)

Reader 1: "Blessed are the peacemakers,"
(Hold up fingers in "Peace" sign and say "Peace, Dude", hippy–style. Congregation repeats.)

Reader 2: "For they will be called children of God."
(Point to Reader 1 and say, "You're a child of God!" Congregation repeats, pointing to each other.)

Reader 1: "Blessed are those who are persecuted because of righteousness,"
(Pretend someone has just slapped your face or punched you in stomach – recoil. Congregation repeats.)

Reader 2: "For theirs is the kingdom of heaven."
(Point to heaven and shout "Where God gets his way!" Congregation repeats.)

Reader 1: "Blessed are you when people insult you, persecute you and falsely say all kinds of evil against you because of me."
(Repeat punching/slapping motion, but do it three times, once for each of the persecutions. Congregation repeats.)

Reader 2: "Rejoice and be glad, because great is your reward in heaven, for in the same way they persecuted the prophets who were before you."
(Shout "Owww!" then "Yaaay". Congregation repeats.)

FOURTH SUNDAY BEFORE ADVENT

First reading

Micah 3:5–12

This reading is a study in contrasts – the prophets who are only interested in pay (if you feed them, they proclaim "peace"), and Micah, who is willing to say what the Lord tells him, regardless of the response he gets. So you need two readers to get this across. Here I offer you two ways to present the same reading.

Reader 1: Reads verses 5–7.

Reader 2: Reads verses 8–12 (adding "Micah" after "as for me" to help make the contrast clear).

Alternative version

Reader 1: Listen to what the Lord says:

"Here is what I have to say about those prophets who are leading my people down the wrong road. They are in the prophet business for what they can get. It's as simple as that. You feed them, they tell you what you want to hear – 'No worries. Everything will be just fine.' Cross them though – and they're out to get you.

"So here's what's going to happen to those prophets. Their visions will come to an end – like nightfall. Their day in the sun will be over, finished, done. They will face shame and disgrace, and nobody will pay any attention to them because, even if they ask, they will no longer receive any answers from me."

Reader 2: Now listen to what I say. Me. Micah.

"I still have the Lord's power, I still have his Spirit, I am still moved by God's desire for justice. And so I have to tell God's people that they are going the wrong way, that what they do displeases the Lord.

"So hear me, leaders of Israel: you who despise justice, you who distort all that is right, you who build your city on violence and evil.

"Listen to what I say.

"Your judges are corrupt, swayed by bribes.

"Your priests are only interested in their paychecks

"And your prophets are like cheap fortune-tellers, concerned with nothing more than the coins you put in their hands.

"It's all about the money.

"And yet, they still claim to hear from God, to be his messengers. 'Surely God is with us,' they say. 'No harm will come our way.'

"And therefore, because of you, your land will be turned over and ploughed under, like a farmer ploughs his field. Jerusalem will be demolished, nothing but a pile of rubble. And on the hill where the temple stands, weeds and thorns will grow."

Gospel

Matthew 24:1–14

The story starts with a bit of sightseeing.

Jesus is leaving the temple, when his disciples start going on and on about the beauty of the temple buildings.

"Aren't they amazing, Jesus?" they say. And "Did anyone bring a camera?"

But Jesus shuts them right up with his response.

"Take a close look," he says. "Because one day – and I'm telling you the truth here – one day, not one of these stones will be left standing on another. It's all going to come tumbling down."

It continues with a question.

Later, when they are on the Mount of Olives, the disciples come to Jesus and ask him to explain. And because they recognize the seriousness of what he's said, it's all very hush-hush.

"That business with the temple," they ask. "When's it going to happen? And what will be the sign of your coming and the end of the age?"

So Jesus gives them an answer. And it's not pretty.

"People are going to try and trick you," he says. "Many will come, and many will say I have sent them, and many will claim to be the Messiah. Don't be fooled by them.

"You will hear about wars and rumours of more wars, but you mustn't be alarmed by that.

"Those things have to happen, but it won't be the end. Not yet.

"Then nations will fight nations. Kingdoms will fight kingdoms. There will be famines here and earthquakes there. But this is all just the beginning of the birth pangs that will usher in the age to come.

"After that, you will be arrested and persecuted and killed. All nations will hate you because of me. And as a result, many will turn away from the faith and will betray each other and hate each other. False prophets will appear. There will be more deception. Wickedness will grow. Love will shrink. But if you stand firm to the end, you will be saved.

"This good news of God's kingdom will be preached to every nation. And then the end will come."

THIRD SUNDAY BEFORE ADVENT

First reading

Amos 5:18–24

I have always loved this reading – particularly the little "story" in the middle about the man fleeing the lion. So let's use two readers and the congregation. The congregation will play the part of the man fleeing the lion, and Reader 2 will lead the congregation in their response to the series of predicaments. Essentially, they just need to scream AAAAAAAH! when they meet the lion, the bear, and the snake. This will need to be explained to them and practised before the reading begins.

Reader 1: Woe to you who long
for the day of the Lord!
Why do you long for the day of the Lord?
That day will be darkness, not light.

Reader 2: It will be as though a man fled from a lion (*lead congregation in AAAAAAAH!*)
only to meet a bear (*lead congregation again – AAAAAAAH!*)
as though he entered his house
and rested his hand on the wall
only to have a snake bite him (*one more time – AAAAAAAH!*).

Reader 1: Will not the day of the Lord be darkness, not light –
pitch-dark, without a ray of brightness?

Reader 2: "I hate, I despise your religious festivals;

Reader 1: "Your assemblies are a stench to me.

Reader 2: "Even though you bring me burnt offerings and grain offerings,

Reader 1: "I will not accept them.

Reader 2: "Though you bring choice fellowship offerings,

Reader 1: "I will have no regard for them.

Reader 2: "Away with the noise of your songs!

Reader 1: "I will not listen to the music of your harps.

Both readers (and perhaps congregation, too, if they have practised):
"But let justice roll on like a river,
righteousness like a never–failing stream!"

Gospel

Matthew 25:1–13

You will need three readers – one to narrate and play the bridegroom and crowd: one to play the foolish virgins (and lead half the congregation in doing the same thing); and one to play the wise virgins (and lead the rest of the congregation).

Reader 1: "Here's what the kingdom of heaven will be like at the end of the age," said Jesus.
     "It will be like ten virgins, with lamps, who went to meet a bridegroom. Five of the virgins were foolish."

Reader 2 *(in a high–pitched voice)***:** Tee–hee, that's silly. *(Half congregation repeats.)*

Reader 1: "And five of them were wise."

Reader 2 *(holding finger in air)***:** E=MC^2. *(Half congregation repeats.)*

Reader 1: "The foolish virgins took their lamps, but they failed to take any oil with them."

Reader 2 *(in a high–pitched voice)***:** Tee–hee–hee, that's silly. *(Half congregation repeats.)*

Reader 1: "But the wise virgins took their lamp and jars filled with oil, as well."

Reader 3 *(holding finger in air)***:** A stitch in time saves nine. *(Half congregation repeats.)*

Reader 1: "The bridegroom took a long time to arrive. And the virgins fell asleep."

Readers 2 and 3: Snore. *(Head on folded hands. Whole congregation repeats.)*

Reader 1: "And then, finally, at midnight, the word went out. 'The bridegroom is here! Come and meet him!' So the virgins woke up and prepared their lamps.

   "The foolish virgins asked the wise virgins for some of their oil."

Reader 2 *(in a high–pitched voice)*: Tee–hee–hee, that's silly. *(Half congregation repeats.)*

Reader 1: "But the wise virgins told them, 'No, we won't have enough for ourselves if we do; go away and buy some more.'"

Reader 3 *(holding finger in air)*: Keep calm and carry on. *(Half congregation repeats.)*

Reader 1: "So off the foolish virgins went. But while they were gone, the bridegroom arrived. And the wise virgins, who were prepared, went into the wedding banquet with him."

   "When the foolish virgins returned, they banged on the door and shouted, 'Sir, Sir, please open up!'"

Reader 2 *(in a high–pitched voice)*: Tee–hee–hee, that's silly. *(Half congregation repeats.)*

Reader 1: "But he told them that he didn't know them.

   "And so I tell you," Jesus concluded, "keep watch, be prepared, because you do not know the day or the hour."

Reader 3 *(holding finger in air)*: Today is the first day of the rest of your life. *(Half congregation repeats.)*

Reader 2 *(in a high–pitched voice)*: Tee–hee–hee, that's silly. *(Half congregation repeats.)*

SECOND SUNDAY BEFORE ADVENT

First reading
....

Zephaniah 1:7, 12–18

You will need two readers – one to read the bulk of the text, and the other to lead the congregation in a "chorus" that I have chosen to weave through the passage. This chorus comes from the text itself, at the end of verse 12: "The Lord will do nothing, either good or bad." I think it summarizes the attitude towards God that the rest of the text counters and seeks to condemn.

Reader 1: Reads verse 7 and 12 up to the "chorus" quote.

Reader 2: Leads congregation, saying: "The Lord will do nothing, either good or bad."

Reader 1: Reads verse 13.

Reader 2: Leads congregation, saying: "The Lord will do nothing, either good or bad."

Reader 1: Reads verse 14.

Reader 2: Leads congregation, saying: "The Lord will do nothing, either good or bad."

Reader 1: Reads verses 15–16.

Reader 2: Leads congregation, saying: "The Lord will do nothing, either good or bad."

Reader 1: Reads verse 17.

Reader 2: Leads congregation, saying: "The Lord will do nothing, either good or bad."

Reader 1: Reads verse 18.

Reader 2: Leads congregation, saying: "The Lord will do nothing, either good or bad."

Second reading

1 Thessalonians 5:1–11

This uses two readers again – one to introduce each section of the passage with a phrase and an action (which the congregation will then repeat), the other to read the text.

Reader 1: "A Thief in the Night – mwa–hah–hah!" (*twirls an imaginary baddie moustache or rubs hands together*). Congregation repeats.

Reader 2: Reads verses 1–2.

Reader 1: "Labour Pains" and "Gentlemen, don't pretend you know what that means!" Congregation repeats.

Reader 2: Reads verse 3.

Reader 1: "Sons of the light – switched on, brilliant, bright!" (*Maybe pretend to switch on a light when you say it, or hold up pretend light bulb and go "ding!" at the end.*) Whatever you do, the congregation repeats.

Reader 2: Reads verses 4–5.

Reader 1: "Asleep" (*head on hands, snoring sound*). Congregation repeats.

Reader 2: Reads verses 6–7.

Reader 1: "We belong to the day – Yay!" Congregation repeats.

Reader 2: Reads verse 8.

Reader 1: "He died for us" (holds out arms in the shape of the cross). Congregation repeats.

Reader 2: Reads verses 9–10.

Reader 1: "So encourage one another" (*puts an arm around Reader 2 or slaps him on back*). Congregation repeats among one another.

Reader 2: Reads verse 11.

CHRIST THE KING
– THE SUNDAY NEXT BEFORE ADVENT

First reading

Ezekiel 34:11–16, 20–24

You will need two readers to emphasize the contrast between how the shepherd treats the two kinds of sheep.

Reader 1: Reads verses 11–16a ("strengthen the weak").

Reader 2: Reads verses 16b, 20–22.

Together: Read verses 23–24.

Gospel

Matthew 25:31–46

You will need three readers: Reader 1 is the king, Reader 2 leads the sheep, and Reader 3 leads the goats. When the sheep are mentioned, their reader says their lines and "Baaa" with them. And when the goats are mentioned, their reader says their lines and "Naaa" with them, if appropriate.

Divide the congregation in half – sheep on the narrator's right and goats on the narrator's left. Then practise making the baaa-ing and naaa-ing sounds, and also make sure you tell them that there were no value judgments involved in the decision about who would play a goat and who would play a sheep!

Reader 1: Reads verses 31–36. *(Whenever sheep and goats are mentioned, Readers 2 and 3 lead their groups in baaa-ing and naaa-ing.)*

Reader 2: "Then the righteous will answer him." *(Leads the sheep in baaa-ing.)* Continues reading the rest of verses 37–39.

Reader 1: Reads verses 40–43.

Reader 3: "They will also answer." *(Leads the goats in naaa-ing.)* Continues reading rest of verse 44.

Reader 1: Reads verses 45–46. (During verse 46, Reader 3 leads the goats in sadly naaa-ing after "punishment" and Reader 2 leads sheep in happily baa-ing after "eternal life".)

HARVEST FESTIVAL

First Reading

Deuteronomy 8:7–18

I think this reading would benefit from two readers, on the one hand to break up the lists of blessings, and to emphasize the point of the passage on the other.

Reader 1: For the Lord your God is bringing you into a good land –

Reader 2: A land with brooks, streams, and deep springs gushing out into the valleys and hills;

Reader 1: A land with wheat and barley, vines and fig-trees, pomegranates, olive oil and honey;

Reader 2: A land where bread will not be scarce and you will lack nothing;

Reader 1: A land where the rocks are iron and you can dig copper out of the hills.

Reader 2: When you have eaten and are satisfied, praise the Lord your God for the good land he has given you.

Reader 1: Be careful that you do not forget the Lord your God, failing to observe his commands, his laws and his decrees that I am giving you this day.

Reader 2: Otherwise, when you eat and are satisfied,

Reader 1: When you build fine houses and settle down,

Reader 2: And when your herds and flocks grow large and your silver and gold increase and all you have is multiplied,

Reader 1: Then your heart will become proud and you will forget the Lord your God, who brought you out of Egypt, out of the land of slavery.

Reader 2: He led you through the vast and dreadful wilderness, that thirsty and waterless land, with its venomous snakes and scorpions.

Reader 1: He brought you water out of hard rock.

Reader 2: He gave you manna to eat in the wilderness, something your ancestors had never known, to humble and test you so that in the end it might go well with you.

Reader 1: You may say to yourself, "My power and the strength of my hands have produced this wealth for me."

Reader 2: But remember the Lord your God, for it is he who gives you the ability to produce wealth, and so confirms his covenant, which he swore to your ancestors, as it is today.

Gospel

Luke 17:11–19

You will need to tell the congregation that they should repeat the reader's action and last line of each verse. You might need a second person to lead them in that.

Reader: He was on his way to Jerusalem
    On the borders of Galilee and Samaria
    When Jesus saw ten men *(hold up ten fingers).*

Congregation: When Jesus saw ten men *(hold up ten fingers).*

Reader: The men had leprosy
    They stood at a distance from him
    And in a loud voice they shouted
    (hands cupped around mouth) "Jesus, Master, have pity on us!"

Congregation *(hands cupped around mouth)***:** "Jesus, Master, have pity on us!"

Reader: Jesus saw them and said,
    "Show yourselves to a priest."
    And as they went to the priest they were healed. *(Look at hands and say "Wow!")*

Congregation: And as they went to the priest they were healed. *(Look at hands and say "Wow!")*

Reader: Then one of the men who was healed
    One of the men, a Samaritan
    One of the men shouted praises to God
    One of the men came back
    One of the men fell at Jesus' feet and said "Thank you." *(Hold one finger in the air.)*

Congregation: One of the men fell at Jesus' feet and said "Thank you." *(Hold one finger in the air.)*

Reader: Jesus looked round and scratched his head
    "Were not ten men healed?" he asked.
    "Where are the other nine?" *(Hold up nine fingers)*

Congregation: "Where are the other nine?" *(Hold up nine fingers.)*

Reader: "The only one who came back," he grinned
    "To give praise and thank God is this foreigner.
    "Get up," he said. "And go on you way.
    "Your faith has made you well!" *(Stand up, arms in air.)*

Congregation: "Your faith has made you well!" *(Stand up, arms in air.)*

DEDICATION FESTIVAL

Psalm

Psalm 122

There are three quotes in this psalm, so I think you will need one reader to read the bulk of the text, and another reader to lead the congregation in saying (or praying!) the quotations. I say 'pray' because that's what the quote in verses 6–7 is – a prayer. So it might be helpful to suggest to the congregation that, when you get to that part, there will literally be a time of prayer, a prayer for peace in Jerusalem – kicked off by the prayer in the psalm, and then perhaps followed by other prayers – prepared ahead of time, if you like, or spontaneous, if that is your tradition. You might want to close that prayer time by quoting the prayer in the psalm again. I think this will really help to bring the meaning of the passage to life.

Reader 1: Reads verse 1, line 1.

Reader 2: Leads congregation in verse 1, line 2.

Reader 1: Reads verses 2–6a.

Reader 2: Leads congregation in verse 6b–7 followed by a time of prayer, if you so choose.

Reader 1: Reads verse 8a ("For the sake of my brothers and friends I will say").

Reader 2: Leads congregation in verse 8b ("Peace be within you").

Reader 1: Reads verse 9.

Gospel

Matthew 21:12–16

Matthew is the only gospel writer to include the detail about the children in this passage. I think it's a great detail and demonstrates that "moaning about noisy children in church" is nothing new. So I think we need to get some noisy children involved in this reading! Use one reader for the narration. Another for Jesus' lines. One more for the chief priests and so on. And, of course, a bunch of noisy children.

Invite some of your children (all of them would be better) to the front and tell them that when you point to them, they should shout, as loudly as possible, "Hosanna to the Son of David!" and jump noisily up. Make sure you practise this with them – it's helpful and fun!

At the end of the reading, once Jesus has made his point (and there is a point, it's not just about noisy children – it's about children and their spirituality and their joy and what they bring to our worship – if we give them the space!) it would be appropriate to sing a song the children know well that gives praise to God.

Reader 1: Reads verse 12.

Reader 2: Reads verse 13.

Reader 1: Reads verses 14–15 up to "in the temple area."

Children: Shout "Hosanna to the Son of David".

Reader 3: Reads from "they were indignant" (at the end of verse 15) to "they asked him" (verse 16).

Reader 2: Reads to the end of verse 16.

First reading

Revelation 21:9–14

This is a nice counting story – so use one reader to introduce the number that frames each section and lead the congregation in a bit of counting, and use the other reader to read the text. As ever, you need to explain to everyone what you're up to!

Reader 1: Seven, let's count to seven! *(Leads the congregation in counting to seven.)*

Reader 2: There were seven angels, with seven bowls, filled with the seven last plagues. And one of them invited me to come and see the bride, the wife of the Lamb.

He carried me, by the Spirit, to a high mountain. And there I saw the Holy City, Jerusalem, coming down out of heaven from God.

It shone with God's glory, brilliant as a jewel, like jasper, crystal-clear.

Reader 1: Twelve, let's count to twelve! *(Everyone counts to twelve.)*

Reader 2: Twelve gates. Twelve angels. Twelve tribes.

The city had a high wall with twelve gates, and twelve angels at the gates. And on the gates were written the names of Israel's twelve tribes.

Reader 1: Now three, let's count to three. *(Everyone counts to three.)*

Reader 2: The gates were spread evenly around the city. Three on the east, three on the north. Three on the south and on the west.

Reader 1: And now it's twelve again. Let's count to twelve. *(Everyone counts to twelve.)*

Reader 2: And finally the wall, the great wall of the city had twelve foundations. And on the foundations were the names of the twelve apostles of the Lamb.

Scripture Index

Anyone Can Tell a Bible Story

Bob Hartman has an enviable reputation as a performance storyteller. Here are his insights into how to retell Bible stories – plus 35 stories to practise on.

"Biblical storytelling can do one of two things," says Bob. "It can excite and inspire and create a thirst for more. Or it can bore and embarrass and leave a group with a sad sense of 'so what?' And that's an important difference, if you believe, as I do, that those stories contain something essential about who we are and who God is."

Good storytelling, Bob explains, comes from blending your own passion, wit and creativity with skill. This book shares the secrets of the skill!

This is a revised and expanded edition of *Anyone Can Tell a Story*, first published in 2002, with many new stories and ideas.

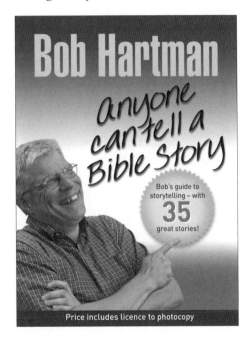

"In restoring the lost art of storytelling, this man has made the Bible accessible to thousands. And now he shares his secrets with us. I picked up so many tips. No more boring church. Let's inspire the nation. If you could kill to tell a story like Bob Hartman, buy his book instead."

– Michele Guinness

Includes licence to photocopy

ISBN 978-0-85721-007-4 £10.99 UK/$16.99 US

www.lionhudson.com/monarch